craft **workshop**

wood

craft **workshop**

wood

25 beautiful step-by-step projects using framework, veneers, carving and simple carpentry skills

Sally and Stewart Walton

photography by Peter Williams

southwater

745.51

This edition is published by Southwater

Southwater is an imprint of Anness Publishing Ltd
Hermes House, 88–89 Blackfriars Road, London SE1 8HA
tel. 020 7401 2077; fax 020 7633 9499
www.southwaterbooks.com; info@anness.com

© Anness Publishing Ltd 1999, 2003

UK agent: The Manning Partnership Ltd
6 The Old Dairy, Melcombe Road, Bath BA2 3LR
tel. 01225 478444; fax 01225 478440; sales@manning-partnership.co.uk

UK distributor: Grantham Book Services Ltd
Isaac Newton Way, Alma Park Industrial Estate, Grantham, Lincs NG31 9SD
tel. 01476 541080; fax 01476 541061; orders@gbs.tbs-ltd.co.uk

North American agent/distributor: National Book Network
4501 Forbes Boulevard, Suite 200, Lanham, MD 20706
tel. 301 459 3366; fax 301 429 5746; www.nbnbooks.com

Australian agent/distributor: Pan Macmillan Australia
Level 18, St Martins Tower, 31 Market St, Sydney, NSW 2000
tel. 1300 135 113; fax 1300 135 103;
customer.service@macmillan.com.au

New Zealand agent/distributor: David Bateman Ltd
30 Tarndale Grove, Off Bush Road, Albany, Auckland
tel. (09) 415 7664; fax (09) 415 8892

A CIP catalogue record for this book is available from the
British Library.

Publisher: Joanna Lorenz
Project Editor: Emma Clegg
Copy Editor: Beverly Jollands
Photographer: Peter Williams
Stylist: Georgina Rhodes
Step Photographer: Rodney Forte
Designer: Lilian Lindblom
Illustrators: Madeleine David and Robert Highton
Production: Sarah Tucker
Reader: Diane Ashmore

Previously published as *New Crafts: Woodcraft*

10 9 8 7 6 5 4 3 2 1

Publisher's Note
The authors and publishers have made every effort to ensure that all the instructions in
this book are accurate and safe and therefore cannot accept liability for any resulting injury,
damage or loss to persons or property however it may arise.

CONTENTS

INTRODUCTION	6
A HISTORY OF WOODCRAFT	8
GALLERY	10
MATERIALS	16
TOOLS & EQUIPMENT	18
BASIC TECHNIQUES	20
MOSAIC KEEPSAKE	24
FISH HOOK	26
SEED BOX	28
CONTEMPORARY SHELF	31
MAPLE CLOCK	34
WAVE WASTEPAPER BIN	37
HARLEQUIN BOOK END	40
FRUITBOX LAMPBASE	42
ANIMAL PRINT BOXES	44
BIRD DRAWER HANDLES	46
MARQUETRY NUMBER PLAQUE	48
CHIP CARVED FRAME	51
FLYING DUCKS	54
MODEL TOWNSCAPE	56
SWEDISH POKERWORK CUPBOARD	60
COUNTRY-STYLE PELMET	62
LONDON BUS PHOTOGRAPH FRAME	64
FISH FACE CUPBOARD	66
DISPLAY STAND	69
FIVE-BOARD BENCH	72
RAINFOREST CURTAIN RAIL	76
ZEBRA RODEO	78
SPINDLE FRAME	82
BOLTED COFFEE TABLE	84
TOMATO DRAWERS	88
TEMPLATES	91
SUPPLIERS & ACKNOWLEDGEMENTS	95
INDEX	96

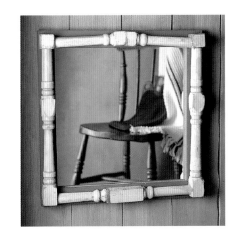

INTRODUCTION

BEING CREATIVE WITH WOOD CAN RESULT IN ANYTHING FROM A COLLECTION OF DRIFTWOOD CASUALLY STACKED IN THE CORNER OF A MINIMALIST APARTMENT TO AN EXQUISITELY CARVED INDIAN TEMPLE SCREEN THAT HAS TAKEN A TEAM OF CRAFTSMEN MANY YEARS TO COMPLETE. THIS BOOK CONTAINS A RANGE OF VERY APPROACHABLE WOODWORKING PROJECTS, TEN BY THE AUTHORS AND THE REMAINING ONES BY FOUR DIFFERENT CONTRIBUTORS. TAKING INSPIRATION FROM NEW AND TRADITIONAL PIECES, THEY ARE DESIGNED TO APPEAL TO STYLISH INDIVIDUALS SEEKING A CREATIVE CHALLENGE.

IF YOU ARE JUST STARTING OUT, CHOOSING TOOLS AND MATERIALS CAN BE INTIMIDATING AT FIRST, BUT IF YOU ARE NOT AFRAID TO ASK QUESTIONS, MOST PEOPLE WHO SELL WOOD ARE ONLY TOO HAPPY TO PROVIDE ALL THE HELP YOU NEED. THERE IS A LOT TO LEARN BUT YOU WILL SOON DISCOVER THAT WORKING WITH WOOD IS ONE OF THE MOST SATISFYING CREATIVE ACTIVITIES OF ALL.

Left: Working with wood need not be a complex skill. This stylish collection of projects demonstrates that beautiful and lasting objects with a practical purpose can be simply constructed.

A HISTORY OF WOODCRAFT

THROUGHOUT HISTORY, WOOD HAS BEEN AN ACCESSIBLE, PRACTICAL AND INVALUABLE MATERIAL. THE DECORATIVE USE OF WOOD, WHETHER FOR CREATING TEXTURES, CARVING NAMES OR FOR PRODUCING ACTUAL FURNITURE, DATES BACK THOUSANDS OF YEARS, AND HAS EVOLVED OVER TIME IN A MANNER THAT REFLECTS THE EBB AND FLOW OF SOCIETY'S ATTITUDES AND FASHIONS, AND THE PROFOUND INFLUENCES OF TRADE AND RELIGION.

WOOD CARVING

Primitive man may have confined himself to the relatively coarse results of the adze or chisel, but the ancient Egyptians were more sophisticated artisans, capable of producing fine true-to-life representations of figures, flora and fauna. Viking long-boats were decorated with carvings, and in the Far East, temples and homes were lavishly embellished with carvings of mythical beasts and demons. In Africa, the Americas and Oceania, explorers from Europe found accomplished tribal wood-carvers using carvings to symbolize their spiritual beliefs, or to mimic their scarification practices.

Wood carving in Europe reached a peak of design intricacy during the

Above: Bakuba mask from the ancient central Congo Kingdom, British Museum, London.

Above: Carved door for a granary from the Dogon of Mali, Musée des Arts d'Afrique et d'Oceanie, Paris.

Renaissance, and the Church gave endless scope for this fashion, from decorative tomb effigies, to the more practical misericords and pew hand-holds provided for their congregation. Grinling Gibbons (1648–1720), the celebrated wood carver of the era, was skilled in carving detailed and highly realistic birds, fruit, flowers, leaves and even a famous replica of a lace cravat (see opposite page) – often from lime. Linen-fold carved wood panelling became popular, and the style of furniture began the shift away from large, heavy tables and chairs, often carved from solid oak, to finer jointed or panelled pieces, lighter and more economical of wood.

In the prosperous 18th century, established trade routes to far flung places, superior tools and a swing towards realism together encouraged a period of exuberant and florid design, with the emphasis mainly on furniture. This was the era of Chippendale (1718–1779), Hepplewhite (d1786), Adam (1728–1792) and Sheraton (1751–1806), whose designs dominated the 18th and 19th centuries. Nevertheless, certain communities resisted the ornate fashions, notably the Shakers of New England. They applied

Above: Ointment spoon decorated with plants and birds and the god Bes. The wood is from Memphis New Kingdom c1300 BC, British Museum, London.

Above: Woodcarving of a cravat by Grinling Gibbons, Victoria and Albert Museum, London.

their Puritan ideals to woodwork, developing their own style in unadorned functional furniture, the unique appeal of which relied on form, proportion, exquisite craftsmanship – and the natural beauty of the wood.

WOOD TURNING

The pole lathe was invented in ancient Egypt, but turning only came to the fore in the 15th–17th centuries, when beds featured turned and carved posts, chairs had turned backs and legs, and tables large central supports. During the 18th century, a cottage chair industry developed in Buckinghamshire, England. The turned-leg chair known as the Windsor originated from this era. The Benjamin Franklin rocking chair was the North American parallel.

A pole and bow lathe made most of the treen (small wooden objects) in use from the 15th century. Some treen, such as bowls and simple spoons, were simply turned, while others, such as butter markers or pastry tools, were turned and then carved, often by a second craftsman.

MARQUETRY

Marquetry (and its close relatives inlay and intarsia) has its origins in ancient Egypt, but the art as we know it developed in Renaissance Italy when Dominican friars Fra Damiano de Bergamo and Fra Giovanni da Verona became famous for their genius with wood. There are many examples of Fra Damiano's marquetry in the churches of San Domenico, Bologna and San Pietro, Perugia. Where necessary, these artists achieved colour effects using dyes, stains, and a peculiar solution of corrosive sublimate, arsenic, gallnuts and urine. Saffron stained wood yellow, Brazil wood boiled with unslaked lime and ashes made red, and verdigris dissolved in vinegar, green. With the invention of the fret saw, in 1562, the design could be cut, jigsaw fashion, and then overlaid, instead of inlaid as before.

In the 18th century, France produced some of the world's most famous marqueteurs, including Boulle (1642–1732), Cresscent (1685–1768), Oeben (1720–1763) and Riesener (1734–1806), but it was a German, Roentgen (1743-1807), who became known as the greatest marqueteur of all time. His work, which had unusual perspective and contrast as a result of his skill in dyeing veneers, was commissioned for the courts of Berlin, St Petersburg, and later, Louis XVI.

Marquetry was popular in England too, and was used by Adam and Sheraton, and later the William Morris Company, to decorate furniture. A particular variant of marquetry, Tunbridge ware, appeared in late 17th-century England, and reached a peak of popularity during Victoria's reign. Named after the spa town of its origin, this craft involved gluing together rods of wood – mainly holly, cherry, yew, plum and sycamore – to make a picture which was sliced for mass production. Tunbridge

Above: Marquetry box (detail), English c1670, Victoria and Albert Museum, London.

ware was applied mostly to small items, such as jewellery boxes, needle cases and medicine chests.

PYROGRAPHY

The art of burning designs on wood ("poker work") is an ancient one, and was practised by even the least sophisticated societies. It became very popular in Europe in the 17th century, when it was used to decorate furniture and treen of all kinds. While it was possible, in skilled hands, to create a range of tonal effects using only the hot steel pokers to burn the pale wood to different depths, some craftsmen also used vitriol, sepia and other pigments, as well as hand-gouging techniques, to build up the picture.

Today, woodworking in all its forms owes its inspiration to the designs and craftsmanship of the past. Even the tools have not altered significantly in thousands of years, and a woodworker today would find the tools in an ancient Egyptian or 15th-century carpenter's workshop quite familiar to their own.

GALLERY

THE ANCIENT WOODCRAFTING TECHNIQUES, SUCH AS CARVING OR MARQUETRY, CONTINUE IN A CONTEMPORARY CONTEXT, WITH NEW CRAFTSPEOPLE USING THE ACCEPTED TRADITIONS OF WORKING IN WOOD BUT ALSO RE-INVENTING THEM IN A PERSONAL VISION, COMBINING IDEAS AND MATERIALS AND DEVELOPING NEW, ORIGINAL AND INSPIRING WORK. THE WORK HERE SHOWS BOTH THE PRACTICAL AND THE DECORATIVE APPLICATION OF TECHNIQUES IN WOOD.

Right: ELEPHANT
50 x 70 cm (20 x 28 in)
Douglas fir was selected to suggest the bulk of this piece as well as the texture of the hide. Having been cut into narrow sections the wood was then secured to canvas so that the body and trunk can articulate. Finally the whole beast was torched and wire-brushed to enhance the grain pattern.
JEFF SOAN

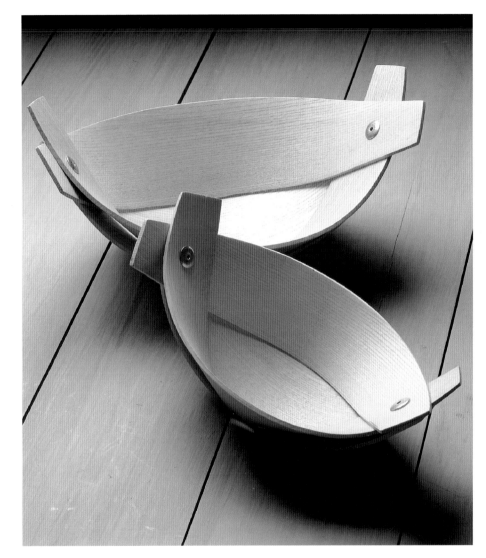

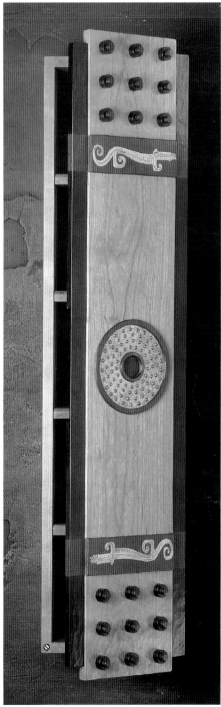

Above: BENTWOOD
BOWLS
An ash tree was cut into
thin boards with a bandsaw
and the boards planed on
one side. The wood was
then manipulated while
freshly sawn and still
green, making it flexible.
All bending was done by
hand on a bench.
JAMES MARSTON

Right: CD CABINET
Height 82.5 cm (33 in)
Made from carved and
stained American cherry,
and inspired by Chinese
bronze work. The dragons
were cut from sheet brass
and etched and inlayed.
The spikes top and bottom
were lathe-turned. The
cabinet is wall mounted.
FIONA CLARK

Below: CHEST
100 x 50 x 50 cm
(40 x 20 x 20 in)
This blanket chest was
made with reclaimed oak,
and even the dowels and
hinges are made of wood.
The interior was limed
and the surfaces left as
they are found or
skimmed with a chainsaw.
WALTER JACK

Right: HERMIT CRAB
ON WHEELS
The six visible legs in this
automated piece (a hermit
crab has two smaller legs
which hold the shell) are
operated by four cranks,
attached by strings and
arranged in alternating
sequence. The wheels,
chassis and base are made
from found woods.
JASON CLEVERLY

Above: LUTE
This lute, made with
cherry ebony and spruce,
is a copy of a medieval
instrument made by
Georg Gerk in 1580. This
instrument requires the
most sophisticated of
timber engineering, the
end result of centuries of
fine tuning.
ANDREW GILLMORE

Left: DROP-LEAF
BIRD TABLES
120 x 60 x 60 cm (48 x
24 x 24 in)
The distinctive carving
and subtle colour of this
work owes much to the
influence of Africa and
India. Drawing from oral
fables, proverbs and
poems, the carvings are
researched by observing
animals' particular and
peculiar behaviour. The
results are an intriguing
combination of the real
and magical. These birds
were carved by hand and
their surface details were
finely tooled with gouge
chisels. Colour was
applied to the carvings
using a water-based stain.
The wood was then sealed
with shellac and beeswax.
NICOLA HENSHAW

Above: DIVING TERN
The piece was made of carved and painted lime. A rough outline of the image was drawn on to the wood. The background was then quickly carved away and the piece developed intuitively, using only four or five different gouge chisels. Finally thinned-down acrylic paint provides the colouring.
KATHRYN O'KELL

Right: WHITE WATER RIPPLE THREE BACK SETTLE
200 x 140 x 45 cm
(79 x 55 x 18 in)
This settle has six drawers under the base of the seat. It was constructed with carved, coloured and burnished spruce and stone handles were attached with leather strips. (Photograph by Amrando Atkinson)
CARL HAHN

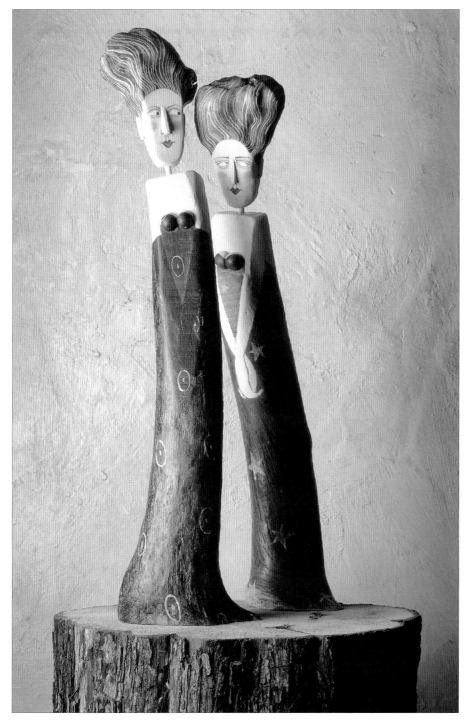

Left: TWO FIGURES
Height 48 cm (19 in)
Made from driftwood
using machine saws, a
sander wheel and hand
tools, the natural shapes
of the found wood suggested
a basis for the figurative
forms. New textures and
grains revealed themselves
as work progressed,
allowing each piece to
evolve. Acrylic paint
provided the colour and
the figures were then
sealed and polished.
LYNN MUIR

Below: THREE BOTTLES
1.1 m (43 in), 65 cm
(26 in), 40 cm (16 in)
Oak was rough-carved
using a side axe, and the
pieces were then worked
across the grain with a
series of gouge chisels. The
final pieces were limed
white, which emphasizes
the textured surface,
before the edges were
softened by being
scorched.
MALCOLM MARTIN

MATERIALS

ALTHOUGH HARDWOODS ARE USUALLY TOUGHER THAN SOFTWOODS, THE TERMS ACTUALLY DESCRIBE THE WAY IN WHICH THE TREES ARE PROPAGATED (SOFTWOODS COME FROM CONIFEROUS TREES) RATHER THAN THEIR WEIGHT AND DENSITY. TWO OF THE VERY LIGHT AND EASILY CUT WOODS USED IN THESE PROJECTS ARE ACTUALLY HARDWOODS – OBECHE AND BALSA. DIFFERENT WOODS SHARE SIMILAR CHARACTERISTICS BUT NO TWO PIECES ARE EVER EXACTLY THE SAME, EVEN WHEN THEY ARE CUT FROM THE SAME TREE. BECAUSE OF THE WAY TREES GROW, THE OLDER HEARTWOOD FROM THE CENTRE OF THE TREE IS FINER AND DENSER THAN THE NEWER SAPWOOD NEARER THE BARK. YOU WILL FIND THAT KNOTS WILL CAUSE PLANKS TO SPLIT IF SAWN ALONG THE GRAIN.

MANUFACTURED BOARDS

Hardboard This familiar brown material, shiny on one side and rough on the other, is made from compressed natural wood fibres and resins. It is easily cut, drilled and pinned and can be painted.

MDF (medium-density fibreboard) A fine compressed board in a range of depths, held together by adhesives, MDF is easily moulded and can be stained, polished and painted. The dust produced by sanding and sawing is dangerous when inhaled, so a mask and good ventilation are essential.

Plywood Thin veneers of timber laminated together, with the direction of the grain alternating, produces a strong board that will not warp. Plywood is lighter than MDF and is availabe in a range of depths. It can be shaped, glued, drilled, stained and painted.

SOFTWOODS

Parana pine The finest of the softwoods, this has a hard texture and is pale golden brown with red streaks.

Red cedar This distinctively scented reddish-brown wood is easy to work and has insect-repellent properties.

Redwood or Scots pine A good all-rounder, this comes in a range of colours from pale yellow to light brown.

Whitewood This timber, cut from fast-growing trees, is mainly used for construction work and economy furniture.

Yellow pine A good quality, fine-textured timber used for mouldings.

HARDWOODS

Many hardwood species have become rare and endangered, so always try to use wood from a renewable source, recycled hardwood, softwood or a manufactured board. Ask your local timber merchant if he has stocks of off-cuts (scraps) that could be used to cut costs.

Ash Pale with an open texture that stains very well, ash can be steam bent and is good for furniture-making.

Balsa This lightweight wood is mainly used for modelmaking. It can be easily cut and laminated to make greater widths.

Chestnut This is similar to oak but much easier to work with.

Lime or linden This is a favourite wood for carving – its grain is really close, enabling highly detailed work.

Mahogany A high quality tropical timber with a reddish-brown colour.

Oak An architectural wood, oak is strong and durable. American oak is softer and easier to work and carve than European. It is light tan to pale grey in colour.

Obeche A lightweight wood with a spongy texture used for packing cases.

Poplar A close-grained yellow wood with a greenish tinge, poplar is easy to cut, shape and carve, and polishes up well.

RECYCLED TIMBER

Drawer bases Old furniture or bureaux, particularly drawers, are a good source of thoroughly seasoned timber for projects. Check carefully for beetle infestation.

Floorboards Usually made of pine, these are found in architectural salvage yards.

Fruit boxes Remove metal staples with pliers and sand the wood carefully.

Stair spindles Ideal for incorporating turned wood into a project if you are without access to a lathe. Reclaimed spindles are inexpensive and can be split in two or cut into shorter lengths for re-use.

OTHER MATERIALS

You will need a range of fixing and filling materials for woodwork. Then, once the piece is assembled, there is a selection of paint or varnish to use.

Nails For a firm fixing (attachment), choose a nail with a length three times the thickness of the wood. Round wire nails with flat plain heads are suitable for most purposes. Oval wire nails are easy to drive below the wood's surface and are ideal for interior joinery.

Paints Water-based versions of most traditional oil-based paints are available, as well as the familar emulsion (latex) house paint and artist's acrylics. Their advantage is that they are fast-drying, have low (little) odour, and are inexpensive. Casein milk paint, also used in this book, is particularly suited to wood and comes in a wide range of colours. Gloss and eggshell are the best-known oil-based paints, traditionally used for all interior woodwork and painted furniture. The oil in this paint has the added advantage of providing long-term protection.

Pins Panel pins have round shanks and small heads, which should be punched below the surface with a nail punch. They are useful for strengthening joints. Hardboard panel pins have square shanks and pointed heads, which do not need punching. Veneer pins are used to secure small mouldings and veneers.

Screws Raised head screws – usually countersunk – are used for drawer handles and other fittings. Countersunk screws have sloping heads, which need a clearance hole and countersinking. Round head screws are used for securing iron fittings. Screws are either steel, brass or coated with black enamel.

Varnish This is either water-, spirit-(alcohol) or polyurethane-based and comes in matt, satin or gloss finishes. Spirit-based varnish, also called shellac, is the best substance for sealing new wood. Polyurethane varnish, available in matt, satin or gloss, and tinted or clear, provides a tough, hardwearing and waterproof sealant, while enhancing the colour and grain. It is smelly, however, and takes a while to dry. Water-based varnish is PVA-(white-glue) based. It is strong, hardwearing and ideal for most indoor uses. It is a fast-drying and low-odour product, which comes in the full range of finishes.

Wood filler Made of sawdust suspended in a PVA base, this is suitable for filling small holes, or wood that is to be painted. It can be sanded when dry.

Woodstain A transparent colour stain that penetrates the wood allowing the grain to show through. Water- and oil-based versions are available and the range of colours grows all the time. Some wood-stains also contain wood preservatives.

Woodwork adhesive PVA (white glue), also known as wood glue, is the standard modern woodworker's adhesive. A light application is applied to both surfaces.

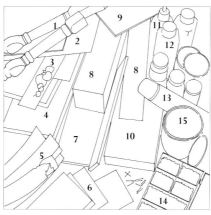

KEY

1 Stair spindles
2 Drawer bases
3 Fruit boxes
4 Floorboards
5 Veneers
6 Manufactured boards
7 Parana pine
8 Obeche
9 Balsa wood
10 Whitewood
11 Woodwork adhesive
12 Paint
13 Wood filler
14 Pins, screws and nails
15 Varnish

TOOLS & EQUIPMENT

WOODWORKING TOOLS ARE SATISFYING TO USE AND, AS LONG AS THEY ARE ALWAYS WELL LOOKED AFTER, THEY SHOULD GIVE YOU MANY YEARS OF GOOD SERVICE. THOSE LISTED HERE WILL ALL BE USEFUL IN A SMALL WORKSHOP. ONLY BUY TOOLS AS AND WHEN YOU NEED THEM SO THAT YOU GRADUALLY BUILD UP A USEFUL COLLECTION. WHEN BUYING, REMEMBER THAT A HIGHER INVESTMENT IN THE QUALITY OF TOOLS WILL ALWAYS MAKE A DIFFERENCE.

Bench hook This flat wooden support for small cutting and shaping work hooks over a bench and has a vertical buffer the other end against which to brace wood, converting a table into a safe bench.

Carving tools Use chisels, straight and bent gouges and V-tools in different sizes.

Chisels The three chisel types, firmer, bevel-edged and mortise, are all made from hardened steel. Polypropylene (plastic) handles are more impact-resistant than traditional wooden ones. Firmer chisels have square blades and are used with hand pressure or with a mallet to chop out joints. Bevel-edged chisels have bevels that allow the blade to reach into corners and cut clean joints. Mortise chisels are the strongest, with tapered blades that are used for cutting deep mortises.

Clamps G-clamps screw up to hold pieces of wood securely between their jaws. They are most useful for holding glued wood.

Drill You will need a basic set of twist bits for your drill to bore holes up to 9 mm (⅜ in). Countersink bits are small and conical in shape and are used to drill wide, shallow tapering holes into which the screwheads can be sunk below the wood's surface. Flathead drill bits have a central point for accurate positioning and a sharp flat shaft for drilling larger holes.

Fretsaw and coping saw These both cut tight curves – the fretsaw is better for thin materials such as veneers.

Hammers Claw hammers are all-purpose tools available in a range of weights. The claws remove nails. The cross-pein is a medium-sized hammer, whose head is

tapered to allow access to small places. A pin hammer is a lightweight tool used for driving in panel and veneer pins.

Handsaw Handsaws have flexible blades with varying tooth sizes and styles.

Jigsaw This versatile saw can be used to cut curves and will also make sloping cuts when the base plate is tilted. It cuts on the upward stroke with the base plate in contact with the wood's surface.

Leather strop Use a piece of an old leather belt for the final stage of tool sharpening. The honed blade is drawn across the leather to give it a sharp edge.

Measuring tape A retractable metal measuring tape is essential.

Mitre saw A saw in a mitring jig allows you to cut perfect 90° and 45° angles.

Oilstone This special stone is moistened with a few drops of machine oil to prepare it for sharpening chisels and plane blades.

Paintbrushes Natural hair or synthetic fibre paintbrushes come in many sizes.

Planes Jack, trying, smoothing and block planes are used for shaving off a thin layer of wood. Generally, they all smooth rough wood, are effective only when well sharpened, and are always used along the grain.

Sandpaper Also called glasspaper, sandpaper is sold in fine, medium and coarse grades. Use it for smoothing rough wood to prevent splinters, rounding off sharp corners and fine finishing.

Craft/utility knife Ensure that you buy the correct replacement blades.

Screwdrivers The screwdriver end should fit the screwhead snugly, otherwise it could slip and damage the wood or

distort the head. The Phillips screwdriver (also known as Posidriv or Superdriv) has a crossed point to prevent slipping.

Try-square and combination square Use these for marking up and checking right angles. A try-square will stand on the work surface on its wooden edge to give a guide for vertical drilling. A combination square can be adjusted for marking out 90° and 45° angles, bevels and mitres.

Workbench This makes woodworking much easier. Choose between a traditional wooden carpenter's bench or the folding multi-purpose DIY (do-it-yourself) one.

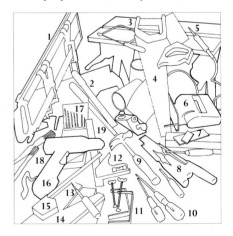

KEY	
1 Mitre saw	**10** Screwdrivers
2 Files	**11** Clamps
3 Workbench	**12** Try-square
4 Handsaw	**13** Cutting knife
5 Pyrography iron	**14** Bench hooks
6 Jigsaw	**15** Tape measure
7 Sharpening tools	**16** Drill
8 Chisels	**17** Drill bits
9 Hammer	**18** Brushes
	19 Metal rule

BASIC TECHNIQUES

A KNOWLEDGE OF THE BASIC WOODWORKING TECHNIQUES, WHICH ARE SHOWN HERE, ENSURES THAT YOU WILL BE ABLE TO MAKE ALL THE PROJECTS IN THIS BOOK. YOU WILL FIND INSTRUCTIONS FOR MARKING OUT, SCORING, USING TENON SAWS AND COPING SAWS, CLAMPING, PLANING, SANDING, SHARPENING AND VARNISHING. IT WILL BE USEFUL TO REFER BACK TO THESE PAGES IF NECESSARY WHILE YOU ARE FOLLOWING THE SPECIFIC STEP-BY-STEP INSTRUCTIONS.

MARKING OUT

1 To mark right angles, use a try-square or combination square set at 90°. Push the square up against the edge of the wood and use a sharp pencil to draw a straight line as a cutting guide. Reposition the square to continue the line on both edges and the back.

2 Mitred edges are cut individually when the face of the wood is different from the back, as it is, for example, on a rebated moulding. This is done using a combination square on the 45° side and a sharp pencil. This wood has been marked for one mitre to be cut, then the square has been flipped over to mark a second one.

SCORING WITH A KNIFE

Using a sharp knife and a metal rule, make a shallow cut along a marked line as a guide for chiselling out a mortise or rebate. Go over the cut several times to give a clean scored line.

USING A TENON SAW WITH A BENCH HOOK

Place the front edge of the bench hook over the nearest work surface and brace the wood into the back edge. Hold the wood with one hand so that the saw blade can be lined up with the other along the side of the bench hook and guided by it to cut a straight edge at a right angle.

CUTTING ALONG THE GRAIN WITH A TENON SAW

Wood should be held firmly in the vice for this task. A tenon saw has fine teeth and the back limits the depth to which it can cut. Pull the sawblade towards you first, then away from you to make the first cut.

USING A COPING SAW

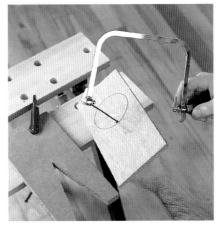

A coping saw can be used to make internal cuts where the edges remain intact. Drill a hole to hold the detached saw blade. Once in position, place the saw handle on to the blade.

PROTECTING WOOD WHEN CLAMPING

If they are to work efficiently, clamps need to be screwed up tightly and can mark the surface of the wood. Insert a piece of scrap wood between the metal and your work to prevent damage.

MAKING GUIDE HOLES FOR DRILLING

The circular motion of a drill can cause the tip of the bit to skid sideways as you start drilling. Avoid this by first making a small hole with a bradawl to guide the tip.

USING A BENCH STOP

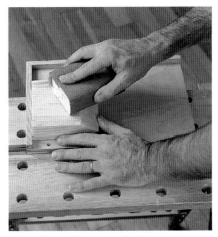

A bench stop has a raised edge on two sides and hooks over the front edge of the work surface, like a bench hook. It provides a useful brace for wood when sanding.

USING A PLANE

The wood must be firmly held in a vice or against a bench stop because you need both hands to operate the plane. The blade should be adjusted to the correct cutting depth and must be razor sharp. The plane cuts as you push it away from you and, although it takes time to master, when you get it right this is one of the most satisfying and effective woodworking tools.

USING CHISELS

Chisels are used to cut away at wood and are either struck with a mallet or pushed into the wood. To chisel out a joint or channel, score the perimeter of the area to cut with a sharp craft knife, then make a saw cut at each end and several in between to control the size of the cuts.

USING A SANDING BLOCK

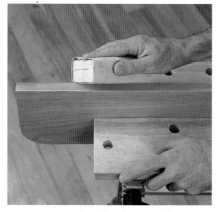

Wrap a piece of sandpaper around scrapwood or a cork block to make a rigid sanding block, and use it for the controlled removal of rough or sharp edges.

SHARPENING BLADES

1 Placing your blade in a honing guide will hold the blade at the correct angle for sharpening. Brace the oilstone against a bench stop, having first of all lubricated it with a few drops of machine oil, and then push the blade backwards and forwards along the stone.

2 When the blade has been sharpened on one side, it will form a burr or wire edge on the other. Turn the blade over and run it along the oilstone to remove the burr.

3 Place the leather strop face up on the bench stop and lubricate it slightly with a few drops of oil. Hold the sharpened blade on the strop at the honed angle, then draw it towards you five or six times using a firm pressure.

PANEL PINS IN MOULDINGS

Snip the tips off panel pins before you hammer them in to prevent the moulding from splitting. It will be easier to manage if you knock them in part-way along the whole length of the moulding before fixing it in position.

VARNISHING

1 Load the brush and apply a good dollop of varnish to the centre of the surface. Spread this out in all directions with the brush to cover the whole surface.

2 Slightly angle the wood at this stage and before the varnish begins to dry go over the surface again using the brush in a more controlled way. Drag it over the varnish lengthwise and then crosswise to give a smooth and regular finish.

USING WORKING DRAWINGS

Working drawings are used for woodworking projects that involve the basic construction of wood (for example the Five-board bench shown right) where precise measurements of the piece need to be recorded. These drawings show the side view, the top view and the end view of the piece. Solid lines show the outlines of the edges as you see them and broken lines indicate the position of the hidden pieces, so that you cn see how the pieces are joined. If you would like to vary the scale of the project, the measurements shown on these working drawings can be scaled up or down.

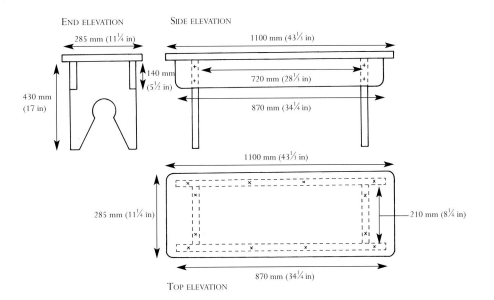

END ELEVATION

285 mm (11¼ in)

430 mm (17 in)

SIDE ELEVATION

1100 mm (43⅓ in)

140 mm (5½ in)

720 mm (28⅓ in)

870 mm (34¼ in)

1100 mm (43⅓ in)

285 mm (11¼ in)

210 mm (8¼ in)

870 mm (34¼ in)

TOP ELEVATION

MOSAIC KEEPSAKE

THIS KEEPSAKE HARKS BACK TO THOSE ROMANTIC DAYS WHEN YOUNG MEN CARVED LOVE TOKENS FOR THE GIRLS OF THEIR DREAMS. THESE DAYS ROMANTIC INTENTIONS ARE MORE LIKELY TO BE SIGNALLED BY BUYING FLOWERS THAN BY WHITTLING AND WOODCARVING, WHICH USUALLY INVOLVE A LOT OF TIME AND SKILL. NOT IF YOU USE BALSA WOOD, THOUGH, AS THIS LIGHTWEIGHT WOOD CAN BE CUT WITH A CRAFT KNIFE, GLUED WITH WOOD GLUE, ROUNDED OFF WITH SANDPAPER AND PAINTED WITH WATER-BASED PAINT. IT'S ALL SO QUICK AND THE FINISHED CARD IS LIGHT ENOUGH TO BE SENT THROUGH THE POST.

1 Measure and cut out two 200 mm (8 in) lengths from the strip of balsa. Apply a thin coating of wood glue along one long edge of each, then join them with a rubbing movement to create a suction. Tape tightly across the join on the back and front, then wipe away any excess wood glue with a damp cloth. Leave overnight to bond.

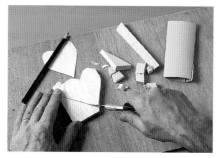

2 Trace a simple heart shape and copy it on to a scrap of wood 10 mm (½ in) thick. Cut it out using a series of short cuts around the curves. Round off the edges with sandpaper, then paint the heart bright red.

3 Cut out 22 large mosaic tiles, about 25 x 20 mm (1 x ¾ in) and 22 small ones about 10 x 12 mm (½ x ⅝ in). The shapes should not be too regular.

4 Paint the tiles using five or six bright colours. Leave to dry, then varnish all the coloured pieces, including the heart, using a polyurethane varnish, which will stop the colour spreading. Varnish the base with a tinted varnish to enhance the colour of the wood and leave it to dry.

5 Spread a dab of wood glue on the tile backs. Arrange the larger ones around the edge of the card, then add the smaller ones and finally the large red heart.

MATERIALS AND EQUIPMENT YOU WILL NEED
100 x 400 MM (4 x 16 IN) STRIP OF 5 MM (¼ IN) BALSA WOOD • RULER • PENCIL • CRAFT KNIFE WITH PRECISION CARVING BLADE • CUTTING MAT • WOOD GLUE • MASKING TAPE • CLOTH • TRACING PAPER • BALSA WOOD OFF-CUTS (SCRAPS) • SANDPAPER • BRIGHTLY COLOURED WATERCOLOUR INKS • PAINTBRUSH • POLYURETHANE VARNISH, CLEAR AND TINTED

FISH HOOK

Y OU CAN NEVER REALLY HAVE TOO MANY HOOKS. THIS FISHY CHARACTER WOULD BE EQUALLY USEFUL IN A BATHROOM, KITCHEN OR HALLWAY OR ANYWHERE, IN FACT, THAT WOULD BENEFIT FROM A LITTLE ORGANIZATION.

IT WAS INSPIRED BY ONE OF THOSE OLD-FASHIONED HANGING SHOP SIGNS AND COULD BE DECORATED IN ANY PATTERN OF YOUR CHOICE. CUT OUT THE ROUGH SHAPE WITH A POWER TOOL, THEN SHAPE IT BY HAND USING A FILE AND SANDPAPER.

1 Trace the fish in the photograph to make a template, enlarge as required and transfer to the poplar. Cut out the rough shape using a jigsaw. Wear a face-mask as protection from dust particles.

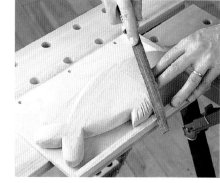

3 Place the fish on a bench stop and use a round file to make the markings. Start with a gentle friction to create a groove, then gradually increase its depth.

5 Use a flathead drill bit to make a hole for the button eye and a 2.5 mm (⅛ in) bit to drill holes for the hooks on the underside of the fish.

2 Clamp the shape in a vice. Round off the edges with a rasp to a 45° angle, blending the angle into the surface.

4 Make parallel cuts for the fins and tail, cross-hatch them to make the belly scales and sand the edges smooth.

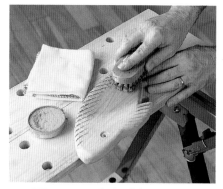

6 Wax or varnish the fish. Leave to dry, then screw the hooks into the drilled holes. Glue on the button eye.

MATERIALS AND EQUIPMENT YOU WILL NEED

PAPER FOR TEMPLATE • PENCIL • 140 x 330 MM (5½ x 13 IN) POPLAR WOOD 25 MM (1 IN) THICK • FACEMASK • JIGSAW • VICE • RASP • BENCH STOP • ROUND FILE • SANDPAPER • DRILL WITH FLATHEAD DRILL BIT AND 2.5 MM (⅛ IN) DRILL BIT • WAX POLISH OR ACRYLIC VARNISH • CLOTH • SOFT BRUSH OR VARNISH BRUSH • THREE BRASS CUP HOOKS • BUTTON FOR EYE

SEED BOX

A PERFECT GIFT FOR THE GARDENER IN YOUR LIFE. GARDENING IS ALL ABOUT BRINGING ORDER TO CHAOS, AND A SEED STORAGE BOX WILL EXTEND THE PRACTICE INTO THE GARDEN SHED. ALL THE SEEDS IN A PACKET ARE RARELY USED UP IN ONE SEASON AND MOST VARIETIES ARE NOW PACKAGED IN SMALL FOIL PACKETS INSIDE THE TRADITIONAL PRINTED PAPER ENVELOPES. THIS GIVES THEM A LONG LIFE AND OFFERS YOU AN OPPORTUNITY TO MAKE A DECORATIVE WOODEN CONTAINER TO KEEP THEM SAFE. THE BOX CONSTRUCTION IS BASIC AND PLANTS PROVIDE THE INSPIRATION FOR THE DECORATION.

1 From the planed timber, and wearing a face mask, cut two sides 250 x 145 mm (10 x 5¾ in); the front 100 x 125 mm (4 x 5 in); the back 140 x 145 mm (5½ x 5¾ in). From 8 mm (⅜ in) exterior ply, cut the base 270 x 140 mm (10½ x 5½ in) and cut the lid 260 x 135 mm (10¹⁄₁₆ x 5¼ in).

3 Score the edges of the rebate using a sharp knife.

4 Using the bench stop, make chisel marks every 5 mm (¼ in) or so along the line of the rebate.

2 Draw a 10 mm (½ in) rebate 10 mm (½ in) down from the top edge on the sides and back to house the sliding top.

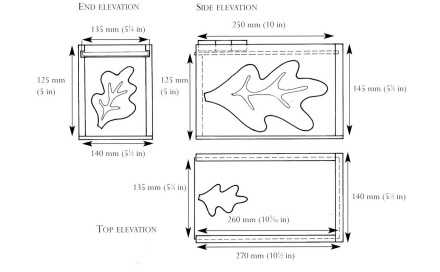

END ELEVATION

135 mm (5¼ in)

125 mm (5 in)

140 mm (5½ in)

SIDE ELEVATION

250 mm (10 in)

125 mm (5 in)

145 mm (5¾ in)

135 mm (5¼ in)

140 mm (5½ in)

260 mm (10¹⁄₁₆ in)

TOP ELEVATION

270 mm (10½ in)

▶

MATERIALS AND EQUIPMENT YOU WILL NEED

900 MM (3 FT) LENGTH OF PLANED TIMBER 150 x 18 MM (6 x ¾ IN) • TRY-SQUARE • PENCIL • FACE MASK • TENON SAW • 8 MM (⅜ IN) EXTERIOR PLYWOOD • SHARP KNIFE • METAL RULER • BENCH STOP • 1 CM (½ IN) CHISEL • HAMMER • SANDPAPER • WOOD GLUE • PANEL PINS • SCRAP WOOD, 1 CM (½ IN) THICK • COPING SAW OR FRETSAW • G-CLAMP • HARDBOARD • DRILL AND DRILL BIT • GREEN-TINTED VARNISH • PAINTBRUSH

5 Chisel out the rebates and remove any rough edges with sandpaper.

7 Sand all the edges, making sure the lid slides well.

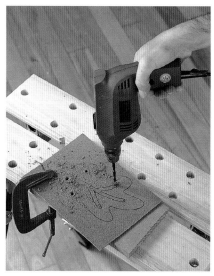

9 Make two large and two small leaves in hardboard. Copy the shapes on the hardboard and drill a hole at each marked cross to accommodate the saw blade. Cut out the inner and outer shapes with a coping saw or fretsaw.

6 Glue and pin together the box sides and base.

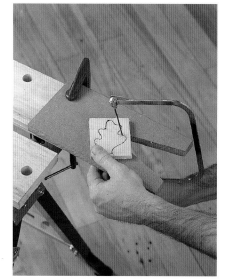

8 Copy the small leaf shape at the back of the book on to a piece of scrap wood about 10 mm (½ in) thick and cut out with a coping saw or fretsaw. Glue to one end of the lid to form a handle.

10 Glue and nail the four leaf shapes to the sides and ends of the box. Then finish the box with a coat of green-tinted varnish.

CONTEMPORARY SHELF

T HE CLEAN LINES OF THIS SHELF ARE AN EXAMPLE OF A CONTEMPORARY APPROACH TO DECORATING WOOD. COLOUR AND TEXTURE ARE USED TO DELINEATE THE COMPARTMENTS AND THIS GIVES THE EMPTY SHELF A SCULPTURAL QUALITY, WHICH CHANGES AS YOU MOVE PAST IT. A MINIMALIST WOULD HANG THE SHELF ON A PURE WHITE WALL AND USE IT TO DISPLAY A GLASS OF WATER AND A GERBERA. A MORE PRACTICAL USE MIGHT BE AS A BATHROOM SHELF.

1 Cut a 600 mm (24 in) length from the plank for the shelf base and a 450 mm (18 in) length for the top. Split the shorter section to get a 100 mm (4 in) wide length with an organic shape. Sand and round off all edges to avoid any potential splinters.

3 Measure 120 mm (4¾ in) from each end of the lower shelf. Place the box backs against the shelf and mark the area to be removed from the shelf.

4 Make several sawcuts in this area and chisel out the waste wood.

2 Wearing a face mask, cut the two box components from MDF. Using a mitre block and tenon saw, cut four pieces 75 x 130 mm (3 x 5 in) and two pieces 75 x 150 mm (3 x 6 in). Cut four 130 mm (5 in) lengths of moulding.

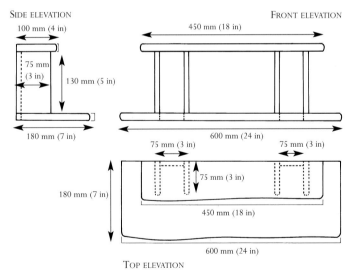

SIDE ELEVATION — 100 mm (4 in), 75 mm (3 in), 130 mm (5 in), 180 mm (7 in)

FRONT ELEVATION — 450 mm (18 in), 600 mm (24 in)

TOP ELEVATION — 75 mm (3 in), 75 mm (3 in), 75 mm (3 in), 180 mm (7 in), 450 mm (18 in), 600 mm (24 in)

MATERIALS AND EQUIPMENT YOU WILL NEED

ROUGH OR RECLAIMED TIMBER (AN 180 MM (7 IN) OLD PINE PLANK WAS USED HERE) • RULER • PENCIL • TENON SAW • FACE MASK • SANDPAPER • 1000 MM X 80 MM (39 X 3¼ IN) LENGTH OF MDF, 12 MM (½ IN) THICK • MITRE BLOCK • 1 M (3 FT) HALF-ROUND MOULDING, 12 MM (⅝ IN) WIDE • CHISEL • HAMMER • WOOD GLUE • 25 MM (1 IN) PANEL PINS OR VENEER PINS • PLIERS • CENTRE PUNCH • WOODFILLER • COPPER AND PEWTER ACRYLIC METALLIC PAINT • PAINTBRUSH • DRILL • COUNTERSINK BIT • 25 MM (1 IN) SCREWS • SCREWDRIVER • VARNISH • VARNISH BRUSH

5 Glue and pin the MDF boxes together using 25 mm (1 in) panel pins.

6 Glue and pin the half-round moulding to the front edges of the boxes. Blunt the veneer pins by snipping off the points with pliers to stop them from splitting the wood. Use a centre punch to push the nailheads into the wood, then fill the small holes.

7 Leave the glue and filler to dry, and then sand the boxes smooth. Paint them with metallic acrylic paint, using copper for one box and pewter for the other. Leave to dry.

8 Assemble the shelves, drilling pilot holes first to ensure accurate fixing of the screws. The screws are fixed through the shelves into the MDF. Once the top shelf is in place, finish with varnish.

MAPLE CLOCK

THIS CARVED CLOCK FACE MAKES A GOOD INTRODUCTION TO WOODCARVING AS IT HAS ONLY FOUR NUMBERS, WHICH HAVE BEEN DESIGNED IN A SIMPLE FORM THAT IS EASY TO CUT USING JUST TWO CHISELS. THE TIMBER CHOSEN IS A MAPLE BLOCK SALVAGED FROM AN OLD FLOOR, BUT ANY WOOD COULD BE USED. IT IS ALSO POSSIBLE TO CARVE SOFTWOOD, BUT YOU WILL GET THE BEST RESULTS USING GOOD QUALITY TIMBER WITH A CLOSE, STRAIGHT GRAIN. THE CLOCK MECHANISM IS A CHEAP QUARTZ MOVEMENT, AVAILABLE FROM CRAFT SUPPLIERS: CHOOSE ONE WITH A LONG SPINDLE TO ACCOMMODATE THE THICKNESS OF THE WOOD.

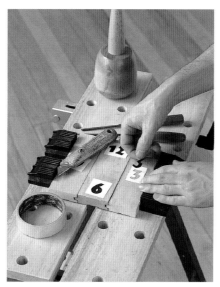

1 Prepare the wood block, gluing strips together if required to make up the surface area. Photocopy the numbers at the back of the book, cut them out and tape them in position on the clock face.

2 Start by marking the outline of the numbers on the surface of the wood, using a sharp knife.

3 Remove the template and, using a straight chisel, cut along the straight edges first. Hold the chisel at an angle so that the cut slopes towards the centre of the number. ▶

MATERIALS AND EQUIPMENT YOU WILL NEED
8 MM (⅜ IN) HARDWOOD FLOORING BLOCK 165 x 165 MM (6½ x 6½ IN)• PAPER FOR TEMPLATES • PHOTOCOPIER • SCISSORS • ADHESIVE TAPE • CRAFT KNIFE • SMALL STRAIGHT CARVING CHISEL • MALLET • SMALL SHALLOW GOUGE • DRILL • SANDPAPER • DANISH OIL • CLOTH • WAX POLISH • QUARTZ CLOCK MECHANISM

4 Use a shallow gouge to do the same around the outside of the curved parts of the number.

6 Remove the wood from inside the number a little at a time until you have completed the form.

8 Drill a hole in the centre of the clock to fit the spindle of the clock mechanism.

5 Use the straight chisel for the inside of the curves.

7 Repeat the process for the other numbers, alternating the chisels as you go around the numbers.

9 Sand the clock face. Oil the surface and, when dry, apply a wax polish. Attach the clock mechanism.

WAVE WASTEPAPER BIN

THIS SIMPLE AND ELEGANT WASTEPAPER BIN IS MADE USING THIN PLYWOOD. THIS IS A NATURALLY FLEXIBLE BUT STRONG MATERIAL THAT IS EASY TO CUT AND SHAPE. POP RIVETS ARE USED TO JOIN THE PLYWOOD AND THESE GIVE A CLEAN FLAT JOIN ON THE SHEET MATERIAL AND ALSO ADD SOME RESTRAINED SURFACE DETAIL. THE BASE IS MADE FROM A PLANT POT TRAY WHICH HELPS TO MAKE THE BIND DURABLE, LIGHT AND SIMPLE TO CLEAN.

1 Working with a file, remove the lip from the rim of the plant pot tray so that the plywood will sit flush with the side of the tray.

2 Mark out the shape of the bin on the plywood sheet, using the measurements shown at the back of the book.

3 Cut out the plywood using a strong, sharp craft knife. Keep your fingers away from the blade.

4 Wrap the plywood around the base, and hold this in position using masking tape. ▶

MATERIALS AND EQUIPMENT YOU WILL NEED

FILE • 25 CM (10 IN) PLASTIC PLANT POT TRAY • PENCIL • METAL RULER • SHEET OF THIN PLYWOOD (LESS THAN 1 MM ($\frac{1}{24}$ IN) THICK) • CRAFT KNIFE • CUTTING MAT • MASKING TAPE • LENGTH OF SCRAP WOOD • DRILL • FINE SANDPAPER • DANISH OIL • CLOTH • WAX POLISH • 3 MM ($\frac{1}{8}$ IN) POP RIVETS • POP RIVETER

5 Mark the positions for the pop rivets along the join, following the curved edge. Support the bin over a length of scrap wood and drill the holes through both thicknesses.

7 Trim away any excess wood from the inside edge at the joint – this will depend on the size of the base you are using.

9 Curl up the bin again, matching the drilled holes at the join, and fit the rivets down the seam.

6 Remove the tape and mark out the holes along the lower edge through which the base will be attached. Drill.

8 Smooth the surface and edges of the plywood using fine sandpaper. Oil the wood and apply some wax polish when it is dry.

10 Fit the base into the bin and mark the positions of the holes through those already drilled in the plywood. Drill the base and attach to the side, inserting the rivets on opposite sides so that the base is evenly attached.

HARLEQUIN BOOK END

WHETHER YOUR BOOKSHELF HOUSES A COLLECTION OF GOTHIC HORROR STORIES OR MEDIEVAL ROMANCES, THIS STAINED AND STUDDED BOOK END WILL KEEP THEM STANDING STRAIGHT, AS WELL AS PROVIDING AN ATTRACTIVE ADDITION. ITS ANGLED CONSTRUCTION MEANS THAT THE WEIGHT OF THE BOOKS RESTING ON THE BASE-PLATE WILL ALWAYS KEEP THE WOODEN PANEL UPRIGHT SO THAT IT CAN SUPPORT A WHOLE SHELF FULL OF BOOKS.

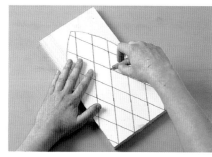

1 Enlarge the template at the back of the book so that it is the same width as your piece of wood. Cut it out and tape the paper to the wood. Draw round the outline and, using a bradawl, make a small indentation through the paper at each point where the diagonal lines intersect. Cut round the shape using a jigsaw and sand the edges.

2 Using a craft knife and a metal ruler, carefully score the diamond grid on to the wood, joining the indented marks.

3 Using watercolours in brown and ochre tones to resemble wood inlay, colour in the diamonds in alternate rows. The scored lines will prevent the colour running beyond the edges of the panels.

4 Leave the paint to dry, then wax the wood with antique wax polish to enhance the colours.

5 Hammer a decorative brass upholstery tack into each indented intersection. The final photograph uses washers placed behind tin roof nails as an alternative.

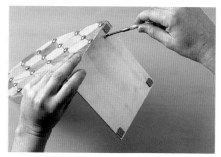

6 Drill and screw the metal or wooden base-plate to the base of the bookend. Stick a cork pad to each corner of the underside to protect the surface it will stand on.

MATERIALS AND EQUIPMENT YOU WILL NEED

PAPER FOR TEMPLATE • 280 x 150 MM (11 x 6 IN) PIECE OF PLANED PINE, 18 MM (¾ IN) THICK • SCISSORS • MASKING TAPE • PENCIL • BRADAWL • JIGSAW • SANDPAPER • CRAFT KNIFE • METAL RULER • WATERCOLOUR PAINTS • PAINTBRUSH • ANTIQUE WAX POLISH • CLOTH • HAMMER • BRASS UPHOLSTERY TACKS • DRILL • 150 x 100 MM (6 x 4 IN) RECTANGLE OF THIN METAL OR WOOD • SCREWS • SCREWDRIVER • CORK PADS

FRUITBOX LAMPBASE

A SURPRISING NUMBER OF FRUIT AND VEGETABLES STILL REACH THE LOCAL STORES PACKED IN BOXWOOD CRATES, WHICH ARE DISCARDED WITH THE SAME INDIFFERENCE SHOWN TO CARDBOARD CARTONS. FOR THIS PROJECT, WE PERSUADED THE LOCAL GROCER TO SAVE SOME CRATES FOR US TO MAKE THIS FUNKY LAMPBASE. BOXWOOD ON ITS OWN IS VERY FLIMSY, BUT IT MAKES AN UNUSUAL AND EFFECTIVE SURFACE FOR A HEAVY COMPOSITE MATERIAL SUCH AS MDF OR CHIPBOARD. THE WOOD SOAKS UP COLOURED WOODSTAIN LIKE BLOTTING PAPER TO GIVE UNUSUALLY BRIGHT RESULTS. MOST BOXES ARE PLAIN BUT IF YOU ARE LUCKY ENOUGH TO FIND THEM WITH PRINTED GRAPHICS, THESE SHOULD BE FEATURED TO ADD A FURTHER DIMENSION TO YOUR DESIGN.

1 From the length of MDF, and wearing a face mask, cut out two pieces 280 x 50 mm (11 x 2 in), two pieces 280 x 65 mm (11 x 2½ in) and one piece 65 x 80 mm (2½ x 3¼ in).

2 Glue and pin the pieces together to make a butt-jointed box with one open end.

3 Dismantle the crates, with the help of pliers, retaining the best graphics. Place individual lengths of boxwood against the MDF and mark them in pencil then cut them to size using a knife and metal ruler. Continue until the sides of the MDF box are completely covered.

4 Glue and pin the decorative pieces in position. Select and cut a piece for the top of the lamp.

5 Use the corner pieces from the crate to make a wide base for the lamp. Measure them against the sides, then mitre the corners. Measure and cut four strips from the crate to make a frame for the top. Glue and pin all the pieces in place.

6 Drill a hole in the centre to take the lamp fitting and another in the back of the base to take the flex (cord). Sand all the edges smooth and finish with varnish.

MATERIALS AND EQUIPMENT YOU WILL NEED

1200 x 65 MM (48 x 2½ IN) MDF, 15 MM (⅝ IN) THICK • FACE MASK • RULER • PENCIL • HANDSAW • G-CLAMP • WOOD GLUE • 25 MM (1 IN) AND 10 MM (½ IN) PANEL PINS • HAMMER • SELECTION OF BOXWOOD CRATES • PLIERS • CRAFT KNIFE • METAL RULER • CUTTING MAT OR BOARD • MITRE BLOCK • DRILL • LAMP FITTING • MEDIUM GRADE SANDPAPER • TINTED VARNISH • PAINTBRUSH

ANIMAL PRINT BOXES

FOR THESE BOXES, THE TRADITIONAL CRAFT OF WOODBURNING HAS BEEN USED IN A VERY UNTRADITIONAL WAY, TO PRODUCE STYLISH ALL-OVER ANIMAL SKIN PATTERNS. THE NATURAL COLOURS OF THE WOOD, AS WELL AS THE SOFT EDGES OF THE SCORCHED SHAPES, MAKE THESE DESIGNS PARTICULARLY EFFECTIVE. EXPERIMENT WITH DIFFERENT STYLES ON A PIECE OF SCRAP WOOD BEFORE YOU BEGIN TO WORK OUT THE DESIGN ON YOUR BOX.

1 Sand a wooden box gently to smooth any rough edges and to remove potential splinters.

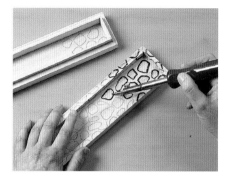

3 Heat the pyrography iron until it is really hot. It will be necessary to stop working from time to time to give the iron time to reheat. Burn the design into the wood, using the pencil marks as guides. Work around each outline with the tip of the iron.

5 Colour the design using woodstain. Paint the inside of each spot with a dark shade before painting over the whole box with a lighter one.

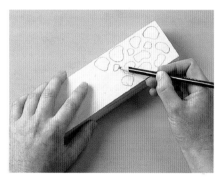

2 Using a soft pencil, draw the animal markings directly on to the wood. Any mistakes can be removed with an eraser.

4 Alternatively, you can burn the whole area to create a design with a different look.

6 When you are satisfied with the colours, paint the box with clear acrylic varnish. Give the wood several thin coats of varnish, sanding gently between the coats if necessary, to protect the colours and give a deep, lustrous sheen.

MATERIALS AND EQUIPMENT YOU WILL NEED

WOODEN BOXES • SANDPAPER • PENCIL • ERASER • SCRAP WOOD • PYROGRAPHY IRON • WOODSTAIN IN DARK AND LIGHT SHADES • PAINTBRUSHES • ACRYLIC VARNISH

BIRD DRAWER HANDLES

A NEW SET OF DRAWER HANDLES PROVIDES AN INSTANT UPLIFT FOR ANY CHEST OF DRAWERS AND IF YOU CAN MAKE THEM YOURSELF, ALL THE BETTER. THESE HANDLES HAVE BEEN CUT FROM 12 MM (⅝ IN) MDF, USING A COPING SAW AND A USEFUL CUTTING GUIDE CALLED A V BOARD WHICH IS VERY SIMPLE BOTH TO MAKE AND USE. THESE BIRD HANDLES MARRY A BARE, INDUSTRIAL STYLE WITH A FOLKSY SHAPE. YOU COULD ALSO DECIDE TO SPRAY THEM WITH A BRIGHT ENAMEL.

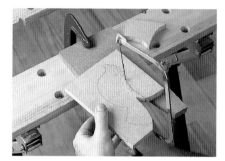

1 Wearing a face mask, cut a rectangle of MDF measuring about 200 x 300 mm (8 x 12 in). Cut a deep V shape out of one short edge. This is your cutting aid – the V board. Clamp it to the workbench or table so that the V is clear of the edge. The piece you are cutting rests on the top and the saw blade moves vertically up and down within the V.

2 Copy the templates on to a piece of MDF. Place this on top of the V board and cut from the outside edge to the outline with a coping saw. Hold the saw blade at right angles to the wood. Cut along the line, moving the MDF to meet the blade. Sand the edges smooth.

4 Use a 14 mm (⅝ in) flat bit to drill countersink holes on the front of the drawer handles to a depth of 4 mm (³⁄₁₆ in).

3 Cut two 20 mm (¾ in) lengths of dowel to sit behind each bird shape. Drill a 5 mm (¼ in) hole through the middle of each dowel and through the bird shape where marked on the template.

5 Varnish all the wood to match or contrast with your piece of furniture. Leave to dry, then sand to give a matt quality and define the edges. Drill 5 mm (¼ in) holes in the drawers to receive the bolts and assemble the handles. Remember to add washers before the nuts.

MATERIALS AND EQUIPMENT YOU WILL NEED

OFF-CUTS (SCRAPS) OF 12 MM (½ IN) MDF • FACE MASK • HANDSAW • G-CLAMP • PENCIL • TRANSFER PAPER • COPING SAW • SANDPAPER • 18 MM (¾ IN) DOWEL • BENCH HOOK • TENON SAW • DRILL WITH 5 MM (¼ IN) TWIST AND 14 MM (⅝ IN) FLAT BITS • MATT ACRYLIC VARNISH • PAINTBRUSH • BOLTS, NUTS AND WASHERS

MARQUETRY NUMBER PLAQUE

MARQUETRY IS A SOPHISTICATED DECORATIVE TECHNIQUE, BUT ONCE YOU HAVE MASTERED THE BASICS YOU CAN TACKLE QUITE COMPLICATED SHAPES TO ACHIEVE IMPRESSIVE RESULTS. THIS DOOR NUMBER MAKES A GOOD INTRODUCTION. IT IS EASIEST TO DRAW SMALL SHAPES, SO USE A PHOTOCOPIER TO ENLARGE YOUR NUMBER TO THE SIZE YOU REQUIRE. IF YOU ARE USING AN OLD FRAME TO COMPLETE YOUR PLAQUE, AS HERE, SIZE THE NUMBER TO FIT IT. MAKE SURE YOU USE A SHARP BLADE IN YOUR KNIFE, AS THIS MAKES CUTTING MUCH EASIER, AND REMEMBER TO USE A GENTLE CUTTING ACTION AS THIS GIVES YOU MORE CONTROL.

1 Trim the veneers to a usable size. Prepare the design for the number and photocopy it to the right size.

3 Tape the veneer for the number on the back of the background veneer.

4 Using a sharp craft knife, carefully cut around the outlines of the number, beginning in the centre of one of the figures.

2 Tape the photocopy to the front of the background veneer.

5 Continue around the number, keeping the knife blade vertical. ▶

MATERIALS AND EQUIPMENT YOU WILL NEED

WOOD VENEERS IN TWO CONTRASTING COLOURS, PLUS A BALANCING VENEER, 160 x 125 MM (6¼ X 5 IN) • CRAFT KNIFE • METAL RULER • CUTTING MAT • PAPER • PENCIL • PHOTOCOPIER • ADHESIVE TAPE • 160 x 125 MM (6¼ X 4½ IN) PLYWOOD, 4 MM (³⁄₁₆ IN) THICK • TENON SAW • SANDPAPER • PVA (WHITE) GLUE • PAINTBRUSH • 2 BOARDS • G-CLAMPS OR WORK BENCH • POLYURETHANE VARNISH • BRUSH • FRAME

6 Cut the plywood to size and smooth the edges with sandpaper.

8 Dilute some PVA (white) glue slightly and brush on to the plywood. Assemble all the components.

10 Clamp the plaque, paper and boards firmly in place, using either G-clamps or a work bench.

7 Cut a balancing veneer to the same size as the background. This has to be stuck to the back of the plywood to prevent it curling.

9 Place the plaque between two sheets of paper, and then place both plaque and paper between two thick boards.

11 When the glue is dry, remove the clamps and sand lightly, being careful not to sand through the veneers. Varnish (polyurethane) the marquetry to bring out the natural colour and insert in a frame. Hang in a sheltered position.

CHIP CARVED FRAME

THIS DISTINCTIVE STYLE OF CHIP CARVING WAS STARTED AS A REHABILITATION PROJECT BY PEOPLE WORKING WITH DOWN-AND-OUTS WHO LIVED ON THE STREETS AND IN THE RAILWAY STATIONS OF NEW YORK AT THE BEGINNING OF THE 20TH CENTURY. WOODEN PACKING CASES WERE DISMANTLED AND MADE INTO DECORATIVE ITEMS, SUCH AS TRINKET BOXES AND PICTURE FRAMES. LAYERS OF THE THIN WOOD WERE BUILT UP TO MAKE THICKER PIECES AND DIFFERENT SIZES WERE STAGGERED TO GIVE AN ATTRACTIVE STEPPED PATTERN. THE WORK WAS GIVEN ADDED COMMERCIAL APPEAL BY BEING PAINTED IN THE PATRIOTIC PATTERN AND COLOURS OF THE AMERICAN FLAG. MOST TIMBER USED FOR PACKING THESE DAYS IS HARVESTED FROM FAST-GROWING TREES AND IS NOT DENSE ENOUGH TO BE SUITABLE FOR THIS TYPE OF WORK, BUT OBECHE IS AN INEXPENSIVE WOOD THAT IS BOTH EASY TO CUT AND RELUCTANT TO SPLIT ALONG THE GRAIN.

1 Measure and mark two lengths 285 mm (11¼ in) and two lengths 240 mm (9½ in) from obeche, for the frame. On the remaining pieces, mark out plain-edged diamonds and squares using a combination square. Cut two diamonds 155 x 65 mm (6 x 2½ in) for the sides and two more 110 x 65mm (4⅓ x 2½ in) for the top and bottom. The largest squares measure 65 x 65 mm (2½ x 2½ in). Three diamonds and squares reduce from these by 7 mm (⅜ in) all around.

2 Cut out the frame using a mitring saw. Mitre the ends of the frame pieces, and sand all the edges smooth.

3 Mark up one edge of a piece of scrap plywood, dividing it into 5 mm (¼ in) sections. Clamp the plywood so that the marked edge overlaps the tabletop. ▶

MATERIALS AND EQUIPMENT YOU WILL NEED
2500 x 65 MM (98½ x 2¾ IN) AND 2500 x 58 MM (98½ x 2¼ IN) OBECHE WOOD, 8 MM (⅜ IN) THICK • METAL RULE • PENCIL • COMBINATION SQUARE • MITRING SAW • SANDPAPER • PIECE OF SCRAP PLYWOOD • G-CLAMPS • CRAFT KNIFE WITH CURVED WOODCARVING BLADE • WOOD GLUE • TINTED VARNISH • PAINTBRUSH

4 Clamp one of the square pieces of obeche just inside the edge of the ply and, using the marks as a guide, make diagonal cuts through the top edge of the wood. Cut halfway into each marked section, keeping the angle and depth the same each time.

5 Now pull the wood forward to overlap the edge slightly and make a series of cuts in the opposite direction. As you meet the cut coming from the other side, the notches should fall away. If they don't, make the cut a little deeper from both sides.

6 Decorate each square and diamond in exactly the same way, then glue each stack together. Clamp the stacks, or place under heavy weights, until the glue has set.

7 Glue the wider frame sections together. The rebate for the glass is made by gluing the narrower frame sections on top of the wider ones, with the outer edges even. Clamp the frame and leave the glue to set.

8 Glue the stacks on to the front of the frame and clamp or tape them in place until the glue has set.

9 Complete the frame with a coat of tinted varnish.

FLYING DUCKS

WOODEN BIRDS WERE ORIGINALLY MADE FOR THE PRACTICAL PURPOSE OF DECEIVING REAL BIRDS INTO FLYING WITHIN RANGE OF THE HUNTER'S GUN, BUT THEY ARE SO DECORATIVE THAT IT'S NOT SURPRISING THAT MANY HAVE ENDED UP AS ORNAMENTS INDOORS. THE SMOOTH, AERODYNAMIC SHAPE OF THE BIRD'S BODY IS SATISFYING TO CREATE FROM A FINE PIECE OF TIMBER, AND A COAT OF ANTIQUE WAX POLISH BRINGS OUT THE GRAIN AND SHEEN OF THE WOOD

1 Copy and enlarge the body and wing templates at the back of the book and transfer the outlines to the pine plank. Mark the position of the eye. Cut out the wing and body using a jigsaw.

3 Shape the wing in the same way, so that the surface curves gently down towards the lower edge.

5 Make an indentation for the eye using a bradawl and glue the bead in place. Polish the wing and body with antique wax polish to give an aged effect.

2 Shape the edges of the body with long smooth strokes of a rasp or metal file. Make the indentations deeper to shape the neck and beak and to give the body a rounded feel.

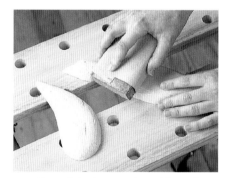

4 Smooth both pieces by rubbing them down with coarse, then medium and finally fine sandpaper.

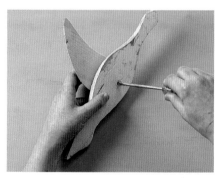

6 Drill a hole through the body and screw the wing in place. Insert a screw eye for hanging.

MATERIALS AND EQUIPMENT YOU WILL NEED

PAPER FOR TEMPLATE • PHOTOCOPIER • TRANSFER PAPER OR SOFT PENCIL • 300 MM (12 IN) LENGTH OF 18 x 150 MM (¾ X 6 IN) PINE PLANK • JIGSAW • RASP OR METAL FILE • COARSE, MEDIUM AND FINE GRADE SANDPAPER • BRADAWL • 5 MM (¼ IN) BLACK BEAD • ALL-PURPOSE GLUE • ANTIQUE WAX POLISH • CLOTH • DRILL • 25 MM (1 IN) SCREW • SCREWDRIVER • SCREW EYE

MODEL TOWNSCAPE

THESE BRIGHTLY PAINTED WOODEN HOUSES WERE INSPIRED BY TRADITIONAL CHRISTMAS ORNAMENTS MADE IN GERMANY, WHERE FAMILIES ARRANGED THEM IN GROUPS UNDER THE TREE ON CHRISTMAS EVE. IMMIGRANTS TO THE UNITED STATES KEPT THE TRADITION ALIVE, MAKING BOTH NOSTALGIC VERSIONS OF THEIR EUROPEAN VILLAGES AND BRIGHT OPTIMISTIC ONES OF THEIR NEW HOMES. THE OTHER INFLUENCE COMES FROM MEXICAN PAINTINGS OF SPANISH-STYLE TOWNSCAPES, WHICH ARE A RIOT OF COLOUR, ROOFTOPS AND ARCHED WINDOWS. THE RESULT IS A FANTASY TOWN OF COLOURFUL SHAPES.

1 Measure and mark off 130 mm (5 in) sections along the length of timber.

2 Cut the timber into short lengths, each one representing one house.

3 Mark the pitched roof. Measure 35 mm (1⅜ in) from the top all round for the beginning of the roof. Mark the middle of the top and connect the points on each side of the block.

4 Place each piece of timber in a vice and saw away the waste, to give a pitched roof shape.

MATERIALS AND EQUIPMENT YOU WILL NEED

MEASURING TAPE • TRY-SQUARE • PENCIL • OFF-CUTS (SCRAPS) OF PLANED PINE PLANKS, 115 x 40 MM (4½ x 1½ IN) • HANDSAW • VICE • MEDIUM AND FINE GRADE SANDPAPER • STENCIL CARD (STOCK) • RULER • CRAFT KNIFE • CUTTING MAT • WATER-BASED PAINTS • PAINTBRUSHES • SPRAY ADHESIVE • PAPER TOWELS • WOOD GLUE • CLEAR MATT ACRYLIC OR POLYURETHANE VARNISH

5 Sand the blocks to smooth the surface and remove any rough edges.

6 Turrets and chimneys can be made from scraps. To get a good fit, place the roof of the house against another wooden block and draw its outline. Cut away the inner triangular shape, then sand the edges smooth.

7 Draw the windows and door on a piece of stencil card (stock), using a ruler to line them up, but actually drawing them freehand.

8 Cut out the stencil using a sharp blade, held at a slight angle. Turn the stencil card (stock) to meet the blade, and when cutting an angle, start with the blade tip in the corner, cutting away from it rather than towards it.

9 Paint the houses in a variety of pretty colours, using any water-based paint you have to hand. Ours were done with a mixture of acrylics, chalky Mediterranean paints and acrylic enamels. Intermix the colours to get a variety of roof and wall shades. Leave to dry.

10 Spray a light coating of adhesive on the back of each stencil to fix them in place. Paint the windows black by first removing excess paint from the brush and applying it with a swirling movement. ▶

11 Apply a thin coating of wood glue to the undersides of the chimney and the roof, then press the two surfaces together, sliding the chimney from side to side a few times to create a suction between the surfaces.

12 Allow the paint to dry for at least two hours, then rub it back to the bare wood on the edges to simulate wear and tear. Rub all over the roof to reveal some of the grain. Varnish the houses with a matt acrylic or polyurethane varnish, which will add depth to the colours.

SWEDISH POKERWORK CUPBOARD

WOODBURNING, OR PYROGRAPHY, IS A TRADITIONAL SCANDINAVIAN DECORATIVE TECHNIQUE. ORIGINALLY, THE WOOD WAS SCORCHED WITH A HOT POKER, BUT NOWADAYS YOU CAN USE A SPECIALLY DESIGNED TOOL, WHICH IS MUCH EASIER TO CONTROL. THIS KIND OF DECORATION HAS OFTEN BEEN USED ON WOODEN KITCHENWARE, SUCH AS CUTTING BOARDS AND WOODEN SPOONS, BECAUSE IT IS SO HARDWEARING. THERE ARE MANY TRADITIONAL PATTERNS, SUCH AS THIS ONE, WHICH YOU CAN USE TO BRING A TOUCH OF RUSTIC SWEDISH CHARM TO YOUR OWN KITCHEN.

1 Copy the template at the back of the book and enlarge it to fit the cupboard door. Rub over the back with a soft pencil, centre the paper within the panel and draw over the outline with a sharp pencil. Remove the paper and redraw the outline to make it clearer.

2 Heat the pyrography iron until it is hot. You will have to stop working from time to time to give the iron time to reheat. Using a pointed end tool, gently burn flower and leaf shapes into the wood.

3 Mark in the dots and circles using round-ended tools, holding the iron at right angles to the box. Add texture in other areas of the design by making small dots with the end of the pointed tool. Smooth the edges of the cupboard with fine sandpaper.

4 Apply the lightest shade of woodstain to the door panel, the darkest shade to the door frame and the medium shade to the outside of the cupboard.

5 Leave the woodstain to dry, then finish off the cupboard with a coat of wax polish.

6 Finish by attaching a brass knob to give a handle for the door.

MATERIALS AND EQUIPMENT YOU WILL NEED

PAPER FOR TEMPLATE • PINE KEY CUPBOARD • SOFT PENCIL • PYROGRAPHY IRON WITH POINTED AND ROUND-ENDED TOOLS • FINE SANDPAPER • WOODSTAIN IN THREE SHADES • CLOTHS • WAX POLISH • SCREWDRIVER • CLOTHS • WAX POLISH • BRASS DOOR KNOB

COUNTRY-STYLE PELMET

AFTER DECADES OF FANCY RUCHING AND FRILLS, CURTAINS AND BLINDS ARE NOW REFRESHINGLY SIMPLE AND UNSTRUCTURED. HOWEVER, A PRETTY WOODEN PELMET WILL GIVE CHARACTER AND STYLE TO AN OTHERWISE PLAIN WINDOW, WITHOUT THE NEED OF A SINGLE FLOUNCE. THIS ONE HAS BEEN GIVEN A SUBTLE FINISH WITH A GENTLE PALE BLUE WOODWASH, BUT FOR A MORE DRAMATIC WINDOW TREATMENT YOU COULD USE VIBRANT PAINT, OR EVEN GILDING.

1 Cut the wood to fit the width of the window plus 200 mm (8 in). Using the template at the back of the book, draw a paper pattern of 100 mm (4 in) triangles to fit the pelmet, evening up any extra space at each end. Placing the pattern on the wood so that the triangle points just touch the edge, draw around it. Drill a 10 mm (½ in) hole at the top points.

2 Using a jigsaw, cut along each marked line from the hole to the edge, to make the patterned border.

3 Smooth the pelmet using medium, and then fine sandpaper, paying particular attention to the insides of all the drilled circles.

4 Cut two 100 mm (4 in) lengths from the remaining wood to make the ends of the pelmet. Sand them smooth and attach to the pelmet with small angle brackets.

5 Cut the moulding to fit along the top edge of the pelmet and glue in place. Leave to dry.

6 Paint the pelmet with a dilute wood-wash and seal with clear matt varnish when dry. Attach to the wall above the window using the large angle brackets.

MATERIALS AND EQUIPMENT YOU WILL NEED

150 x 18 MM (6 x ¾ IN) PINE PLANK TO FIT THE WINDOW • RULER • PENCIL • TRY-SQUARE • JIGSAW • PAPER TEMPLATE • G-CLAMPS • DRILL • MEDIUM AND FINE GRADE SANDPAPER • FOUR 25 MM (1 IN) ANGLE BRACKETS • SCREWS • SCREWDRIVER • DECORATIVE MOULDING • WOOD GLUE • PALE BLUE WOODWASH • PAINTBRUSH • CLEAR MATT VARNISH • TWO 100 MM (4 IN) ANGLE BRACKETS

LONDON BUS PHOTOGRAPH FRAME

THIS INGENIOUS FRAME IS BASED ON THE SHAPE OF THE CLASSIC LONDON DOUBLE-DECKER BUS, BUT THE IDEA COULD ALSO BE ADAPTED TO OTHER SHAPES, SUCH AS A HOUSE OR A TRAIN. IT IS AN ORIGINAL WAY TO DISPLAY PHOTOGRAPHS OF A GROUP OF FRIENDS OR RELATIONS, AND WOULD MAKE A LOVELY KEEPSAKE. THE PICTURES HAVE JUST BEEN TAPED TO THE BACK TO KEEP IT SIMPLE AND AND EASY TO CHANGE. IF YOU'RE TAKING PHOTOGRAPHS ESPECIALLY FOR THIS FRAME, TRY TO GET SIDE-ON PORTRAITS OF PEOPLE SO THAT THEY REALLY LOOK LIKE PASSENGERS INSIDE THE BUS.

1 Copy the bus template at the back of the book and enlarge it to the size you need. Cut a piece of plywood large enough to fit the bus and stick the template to the wood with masking tape. Drill a starter hole for the fretsaw blade in each window of the bus.

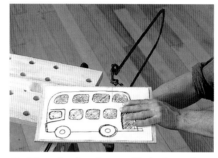

3 Thread a fine fretsaw blade through each starter hole in turn and cut out the bus windows and door. Turn the plywood to meet the saw blade and keep the blade vertical as you cut, to ensure a neat edge.

5 Smooth all the edges of the shape with sandpaper. Using a pencil, mark the wheels and any other details on the front of the bus.

2 Make a deep V-shaped cut in a piece of scrap timber and clamp it over the edge of the workbench to make a V board as a support for cutting out the shapes.

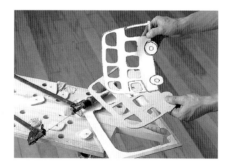

4 Cut around the driver's cab and the outline of the bus, and then remove the template.

6 Cut out a stand and glue to the back of the bus. Leave the glue to harden, then paint the whole frame and tape photographs to the back of each opening.

MATERIALS AND EQUIPMENT YOU WILL NEED

PAPER TEMPLATE • PHOTOCOPIER • 320 x 220 MM (12½ x 8¾ IN) PLYWOOD 4 MM (³⁄₁₆ IN) THICK • PENCIL • METAL RULER • FRETSAW AND FINE BLADE • MASKING TAPE • G-CLAMP • DRILL • SCRAP TIMBER • FINE GRADE SANDPAPER • WOOD GLUE • ACRYLIC ENAMEL PAINTS • PAINTBRUSHES • ADHESIVE TAPE • PHOTOGRAPHS

FISH FACE CUPBOARD

WHETHER OR NOT YOU EVER USE THIS LITTLE CUPBOARD FOR SECRET TREASURES (AND WHO KNOWS WHAT IT MIGHT BE CAPABLE OF CONCEALING?), IT HAS AN AIR OF INTRIGUE AND MYSTERY AND WILL FILL EVERYONE WHO SEES IT ON YOUR WALL WITH AN URGENT NEED TO KNOW WHAT IS INSIDE. THE BASIC CONSTRUCTION IS REFRESHINGLY SIMPLE, THEREFORE GIVING YOU THE FREEDOM TO APPLY THE PAINTINGS AND CARVED SHAPES OF YOUR CHOICE.

1 Cut four lengths of pine each 230 mm (9 in) for the frame. Cut eight lengths of dowel each 75 mm (3 in).

3 Paint the frame with white emulsion (latex). When dry, scrape off the excess with the edge of a craft knife blade, exposing the grain.

5 Carve a simple fish shape in relief, using a craft knife, and sand gently to a smooth curved shape. Then add fins.

2 Near each end of two lengths of frame, drill two holes through the 50 mm (2 in) thickness. Drill corresponding holes in the ends of each of the other two. Secure the sections together using the dowelling pegs and wood glue. Leave to dry. Use a wire brush to raise the grain of the wood.

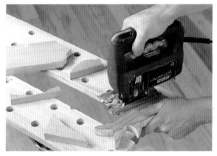

4 Copy your fish design and draw it on a piece of 18 mm (¾ in) thick pine. Cut out the shape using a jigsaw.

6 Measure the frame opening and cut a piece of 18 mm (¾ in) thick pine to fit. Cut a small plywood panel for the door and sand smoothly. Centre the panel on the door and draw around it. Drill a starter hole in which to insert the jigsaw blade and cut out the panel so that the plywood fits exactly.

▶

MATERIALS AND EQUIPMENT YOU WILL NEED

920 MM (36 IN) LENGTHS OF 50 x 100 MM (2 x 4 IN) PLANED PINE • JIGSAW • 8 MM (⅜ IN) DOWEL • DRILL WITH 8 MM (⅜ IN) BIT • WOOD GLUE • WIRE BRUSH • WHITE EMULSION (LATEX) • PAINTBRUSHES • CRAFT KNIFE • TEMPLATE • PENCIL • 150 MM (6 IN) PLANED PINE, 18 MM (¾ IN) THICK • SANDPAPER • 4 MM (1/16 IN) PLYWOOD • REFERENCE FOR PANEL • ENAMEL PAINTS • DARK RED OIL-BASED WOODSTAIN • GOLD SIZE • DUTCH METAL LEAF • MATT VARNISH • HINGES • SCREWS • SCREWDRIVER • DOOR KNOB • GLASS PLATES • 2 MM (2/16 IN) MILD STEEL WIRE

7 Choose an image for the door panel and paint the picture directly on to the plywood surface.

9 Paint the fish in a naturalistic manner, varnish and leave to dry.

10 Press the painted panel into the door – it should fit tightly. Screw on two small hinges and attach the door to the frame. Put a knob on the door. Place two glass plates in the interior of the frame, which will conceal them, for hanging.

8 Paint the door with dark red wood-stain and leave to dry. Brush on a coat of gold size and leave until tacky, then apply Dutch metal leaf. Seal with a further layer of size and leave to dry.

11 Drill holes in the top of the frame and the bottom of the fish and attach the fish with a short piece of wire. Finish by painting the wire.

DISPLAY STAND

Aꜱ ᴛᴀʟʟ ᴄᴏʟᴜᴍɴ ᴍᴀᴋᴇꜱ ᴀɴ ᴇʟᴇɢᴀɴᴛ ꜱᴛᴀɴᴅ ꜰᴏʀ ᴀ ᴛʀᴀɪʟɪɴɢ ᴘʟᴀɴᴛ, ᴏʀ ᴄᴀɴ ʙᴇ ᴜꜱᴇᴅ ᴀꜱ ᴀ ꜱᴜᴘᴘᴏʀᴛ ꜰᴏʀ ᴀ ᴛᴀʙʟᴇ ʟᴀᴍᴘ, ᴍᴀᴋɪɴɢ ɪᴛ ᴡᴏʀᴋ ʟɪᴋᴇ ᴀ ꜱᴛᴀɴᴅᴀʀᴅ ʟᴀᴍᴘ. ᴛʜɪꜱ ᴄᴏʟᴜᴍɴ ɪꜱ ꜱɪᴍᴘʟʏ ᴀ ʟᴇɴɢᴛʜ ᴏꜰ ꜱᴛᴏᴜᴛ ᴛɪᴍʙᴇʀ ᴡɪᴛʜ ᴀ ᴛᴏᴘ ᴀɴᴅ ʙᴀꜱᴇ ᴏꜰ ᴘʟʏᴡᴏᴏᴅ ꜱQᴜᴀʀᴇꜱ ᴏꜰ ᴅᴇᴄʀᴇᴀꜱɪɴɢ ꜱɪᴢᴇ. ꜱᴘᴀᴄᴇʀꜱ ʙᴇᴛᴡᴇᴇɴ ᴛʜᴇ ꜱQᴜᴀʀᴇꜱ ɢɪᴠᴇ ᴛʜᴇ ᴅᴇꜱɪɢɴ ɪᴍᴘᴀᴄᴛ, ᴀɴᴅ ʏᴏᴜ ᴄᴀɴ ᴀʟꜱᴏ ᴀᴅᴅ ᴘʟʏᴡᴏᴏᴅ ꜰᴇᴇᴛ ᴛᴏ ᴛʜᴇ ʙᴀꜱᴇ ɪꜰ ʏᴏᴜ ᴡɪꜱʜ. ᴘᴀɪɴᴛ, ꜱᴛᴀɪɴ ᴏʀ ᴠᴀʀɴɪꜱʜ ᴛʜᴇ ᴡᴏᴏᴅ ᴛᴏ ꜱᴜɪᴛ ʏᴏᴜʀ ɪɴᴛᴇʀɪᴏʀ.

1 Following the plan, mark out the squares for the top and base on the plywood sheet.

2 Carefully cut out the plywood squares, using a panel saw.

3 Draw lines between opposite corners to find the centre of each square and drill a hole in each. ▶

MATERIALS AND EQUIPMENT YOU WILL NEED

Pᴇɴᴄɪʟ • Rᴜʟᴇʀ • 750 x 600 ᴍᴍ (30 x 24 ɪɴ) ꜱʜᴇᴇᴛ ᴘʟʏᴡᴏᴏᴅ, 9 ᴍᴍ (⅜ ɪɴ) ᴛʜɪᴄᴋ • Pᴀɴᴇʟ ꜱᴀᴡ • G-ᴄʟᴀᴍᴘ • Dʀɪʟʟ ᴀɴᴅ 6 ᴍᴍ (¼ ɪɴ) ʙɪᴛ • Mᴇᴅɪᴜᴍ ᴀɴᴅ ꜰɪɴᴇ ɢʀᴀᴅᴇ ꜱᴀɴᴅᴘᴀᴘᴇʀ • 100 ᴍᴍ (4 ɪɴ) ꜱQᴜᴀʀᴇ ꜱᴏꜰᴛᴡᴏᴏᴅ, 1000 ᴍᴍ (39 ɪɴ) ɪɴ ʟᴇɴɢᴛʜ • Wᴏᴏᴅ ɢʟᴜᴇ • Sʜᴏʀᴛ ꜱᴄʀᴇᴡꜱ • Sᴄʀᴇᴡᴅʀɪᴠᴇʀ • Tɪɴᴛᴇᴅ ᴠᴀʀɴɪꜱʜ • Pᴀɪɴᴛʙʀᴜꜱʜ • Tᴡᴏ 6 x 75 ᴍᴍ (¼ x 3 ɪɴ) ꜱᴄʀᴇᴡꜱ

4 Sand all the components smooth, including the softwood column.

6 Varnish the horizontal surfaces of the plywood squares before assembling the column. Leave to dry.

7 Using wood glue and a long screw at each end, assemble the top and base of the column. Align the squares by eye. Complete the staining and varnishing.

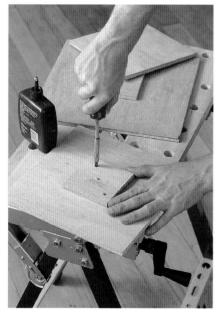

5 Attach a 100 mm (4 in) spacer square centrally to each of the larger squares, using wood glue and short screws.

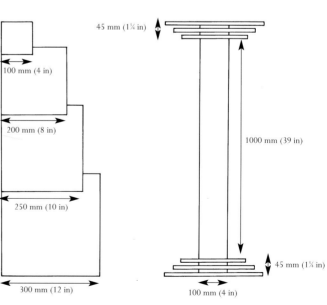

TOP ELEVATION OF LAYERS

100 mm (4 in)

200 mm (8 in)

250 mm (10 in)

300 mm (12 in)

SIDE ELEVATION

45 mm (1¾ in)

1000 mm (39 in)

45 mm (1¾ in)

100 mm (4 in)

FIVE-BOARD BENCH

STRONG AND PRACTICAL BENCHES SUCH AS THIS HAVE BEEN MADE IN THIS WAY FOR HUNDREDS OF YEARS, EVER SINCE IT WAS REALIZED THAT THEY USED A MOST ECONOMICAL AMOUNT OF TIMBER, NAILS AND TIME. THE KEY TO THIS DESIGN LIES IN THE WAY THE STRESS IS SPREAD BOTH HORIZONTALLY AND VERTICALLY, SO THAT PRESSURE FROM ONE DIRECTION CREATES AN EQUAL PRESSURE IN THE OTHER AND HOLDS THE PIECE TOGETHER.

1 Following the working drawing, mark out the five pieces on the wood. Use a pair of compasses to give the circular shapes in the side elevation.

3 Using a suitable guide for the curve, such as a roll of masking tape, round off the corners of the seat and the bottom corners of the two sides. Remove the excess wood using a jigsaw.

4 Sand all the edges smooth. To sand the inner curves, it's a good idea to wrap sandpaper around a piece of dowel or broom handle.

2 Cut out the pieces using a handsaw. Use a jigsaw to cut out the "keyholes" in the legs.

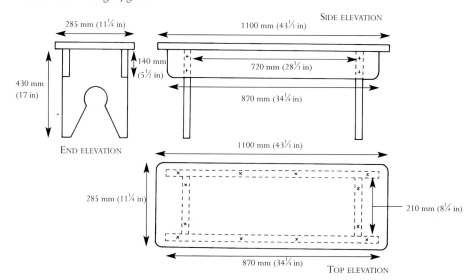

SIDE ELEVATION

285 mm (11¼ in)

1100 mm (43⅓ in)

140 mm (5½ in)

430 mm (17 in)

720 mm (28⅓ in)

870 mm (34¼ in)

END ELEVATION

1100 mm (43⅓ in)

285 mm (11¼ in)

210 mm (8¼ in)

870 mm (34¼ in)

TOP ELEVATION

MATERIALS AND EQUIPMENT YOU WILL NEED

TWO 1530 x 290 x 20 MM (60 x 11½ x ¾ IN) PLANKS OF PARANA PINE • COMBINATION SQUARE • MEASURING TAPE • PENCIL • PAIR OF COMPASSES • HANDSAW • JIGSAW • ROLL OF MASKING TAPE • SANDPAPER • LENGTH OF DOWEL • TENON SAW • CROSSCUT SAW • CHISEL • HAMMER • DRILL AND TWIST BITS • COUNTERSINK BIT • 45 MM (1¾ IN) SCREWS • SCREWDRIVER • WOOD FILLER • MILK PAINT • PAINTBRUSH

5 Mark the rebates in the legs using an scrap of the pine length to measure the width.

6 Cut out the short edges of the rebates using a tenon saw and use a crosscut saw for the long edges.

7 Use a chisel to finish cutting the rebates accurately.

8 Mark the position of the legs on the sides of the bench.

9 Drill the holes on the sides to take the screws.

10 Fit a countersink bit and drill the same holes again. ▶

11 Turn up the side pieces and use a smaller drill bit to make pilot holes for the screws.

13 Fill the screw holes with wood filler. Leave them to dry, and then sand smooth.

12 Attach the side pieces to the legs. Repeat the procedure in order to attach the seat.

14 Paint the bench with milk paint. Once the paint is dry, sand the edges to give a slightly distressed finish.

RAINFOREST CURTAIN RAIL

CUSTOMIZE AN ORDINARY UNTREATED CURTAIN POLE WITH A STRIKING LEOPARDSKIN PRINT. BURNING THE DESIGN INTO THE WOOD WITH A PYROGRAPHY TOOL MAKES IT VERY HARDWEARING, SO IT WILL HAPPILY SURVIVE THE CONSTANT RUBBING OF THE CURTAIN RINGS AS THE CURTAINS ARE OPENED AND CLOSED. THE ADDITION OF BRIGHT YELLOW STUDDED FINIALS MAKE A SUITABLY DRAMATIC FINISHING TOUCH.

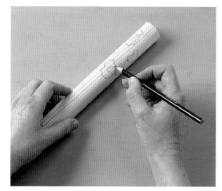

1 Using a soft pencil, draw a series of leopardskin markings along the length of the curtain rail.

3 Paint the pole with a wash of yellow emulsion (latex) paint.

5 Paint the finials and fittings in yellow. When the paint is dry, protect the pole and fittings with a coat of matt varnish.

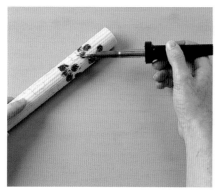

2 Heat the pyrography iron until it is really hot. It will be necessary to stop working from time to time, in order to give the iron time to reheat. Using a pointed end tool, burn long fur-like lines across each shape.

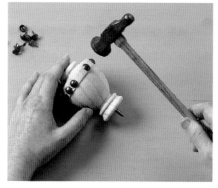

4 Decorate the finials, by hammering in a round of decorative, shiny upholstery tacks.

6 Thread on the curtain rings and assemble the pole.

MATERIALS AND EQUIPMENT YOU WILL NEED

SOFT PENCIL • UNTREATED WOODEN CURTAIN POLE AND FITTINGS • PYROGRAPHY IRON • YELLOW EMULSION (LATEX) PAINT • PAINTBRUSH • DARK METAL UPHOLSTERY TACKS • HAMMER • CLEAR MATT VARNISH

ZEBRA RODEO

THIS FABULOUS AUTOMATED TOY ON WHEELS WILL AMUSE PEOPLE OF ALL AGES, BUT IT IS REALLY STRICTLY FOR GROWN-UPS. BASED ON A TRADITIONAL DESIGN, THE SIMPLE MECHANISM OF THE CRANKED AXLES PRODUCES A FASCINATINGLY LIFELIKE EFFECT. THIS EXAMPLE SHOWS A BUCKING BRONCO OR, WITH THE TEMPLATE AT THE BACK OF THE BOOK, YOU CAN CREATE AN AUTOMATED OSTRICH AND THEN ADD A RIDER AFTERWARDS. THE BASIC RULES OF AUTOMATA ARE EASILY ADAPTED TO ANY PIECE. RESEARCH DIFFERENT ANIMAL SUBJECTS FROM BOOKS OR MAGAZINES.

1 Photocopy and enlarge your chosen animal and figure templates. Using PVA (white) glue, stick the drawing to a sheet of 5 mm (¼ in) thick beech plywood. When dry, cut out the pieces with a non-rip jigsaw blade. Wrap the bed of the jigsaw in packing tape.

2 Using PVA glue, stick some printed sheets or magazine ephemera on to another piece of plywood. When dry, use a 75 mm (3 in) hole saw to cut out four wheels. Sand the edges smooth and fill each central hole with a piece of dowel, using wood glue.

3 For the chassis, cut two 250 x 20 mm (10 x ¾ in) lengths of 18 mm (¾ in) square pine. Drill a hole about 20 mm (¾ in) from each end for the axles. Drill two more sets of holes, at right angles to the others and about 50 mm (2 in) from each end, for the supports. Then push a rusty 10 cm (4 in) nail through each central hole.

MATERIALS AND EQUIPMENT YOU WILL NEED

WHITE PAPER • PHOTOCOPIER • PVA (WHITE) GLUE • 5 MM (¼ IN) THICK BEECH PLYWOOD • JIGSAW WITH NON-RIP BLADE • PACKING TAPE • PRINTED MAGAZINE PAGES • DRILL • 7.5 CM (3 IN) HOLE SAW • SANDPAPER • NARROW DOWEL • WOOD GLUE • 18 MM (¾ IN) SQUARE PINE • FOUR OLD 10 CM (4 IN) NAILS • 3 MM (⅛ IN) MILD STEEL WIRE • VICE • HAMMER • 18 MM (¾ IN) THICK PINE OFF-CUT (SCRAP) • CRAFT KNIFE • PANEL PINS • 1 MM (1/24 IN) BRASS WIRE • WIRE CUTTERS • PLIERS • SCRAP OF 5 MM (¼ IN) PLASTIC TUBING • FILE • EPOXY RESIN GLUE • BLOW TORCH

4 Using 3 mm (⅛ in) mild steel wire, make two cranked axles. It can be bent by hand, using a vice and a hammer. Make sure the ends of each axle will align.

6 Using a small bit, drill the cowboy and the zebra at the points where they will be articulated, ready for assembly.

8 Assemble the cowboy's joints in the same way. Do not connect the zebra's front legs until step 14.

5 From a piece of 18 mm (¾ in) thick pine, cut a platform about 175 mm (7 in) long for the zebra and rider to stand on. Carve the top edge roughly with a craft knife, then finish with sandpaper.

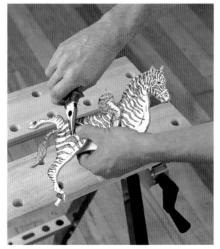

7 Glue and pin the cowboy's legs either side of the zebra's back, making sure they are aligned. Assemble the zebra's back legs with 1 mm (1/24 in) brass wire. Bend an L-shape in one end of a length of wire, push the other end through the holes and bend another L-shape at the other side. Snip off the excess wire, making sure that the legs swing freely.

9 Thread a short piece of plastic tubing on to each axle crank. Put the axles in position in the chassis, then attach the chassis to the platform by drilling pilot holes in the platform and hammering in the nails to secure. The nails used for the supports should look appropriately old: leave them in salt water to rust them.

▶

10 Attach the hind legs of the zebra to the platform with wood glue and by drilling tiny pilot holes through the hooves and hammering in panel pins to secure firmly.

11 To attach the wheels, file down the axle ends a little, then drill a hole through the dowel in the centre of each wheel and secure to the axle using epoxy resin glue.

12 Anneal, or soften, the ends of the brass wire used in the mechanism, by heating them to a cherry red using a blow torch, then cool them in water.

13 To connect the mechanism, anneal one end of a length of brass wire, wrap it around the tube on the rear axle and thread the other end through a small hole drilled in the cowboy's arm. Bend the wire to secure (this must be a loose connection).

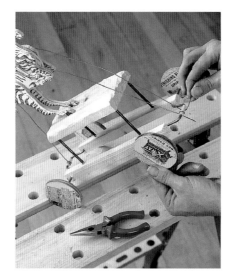

14 For the front legs, anneal both ends of a length of brass wire and thread it through the front legs and body of the zebra. Bend both ends down and wrap the softened sections around the tubing on the front crank.

15 Follow these rules to articulate any image and create your chosen automata subject on wheels.

For example, to use the ostrich template at the back of the book, start by attaching the neck and tail to the main body. With the same method used for the cowboy, make each joint with wire pins and small drill holes. Then run wires from cranks up to the neck and tail. In order to make this work effectively you should check that the "up and down" distance of the wire produces the amount of movement you require. This can be altered by placing the hole at varying distances from the main axis. Do a test first by making several holes at different points on scrap wood.

SPINDLE FRAME

NOT MANY OF US HAVE THE CHANCE TO TURN WOOD ON A LATHE, BUT WHEN YOU SEE IT DONE IT HOLDS THE SAME FASCINATION AS WATCHING A POT BEING THROWN ON A WHEEL. A BOOK ABOUT DECORATIVE WOOD WOULD BE INCOMPLETE WITHOUT SOME WOODTURNING, THOUGH IT DOES REQUIRE BOTH SPECIALIST SKILL AND EQUIPMENT. SO THIS PROJECT MAKES USE OF RECLAIMED STAIRCASE SPINDLES THAT SOMEONE ELSE HAS HAD THE PLEASURE OF TURNING. NEW SPINDLES CAN BE BOUGHT FROM DIY (DO-IT-YOURSELF) CENTRES AND A SIMILAR SHABBY CHIC EFFECT CAN BE CREATED BY GIVING THEM A DISTRESSED PAINT FINISH. ASK THE TIMBER MERCHANT TO CUT A 5 MM (¼ IN) REBATE ALONG THE LENGTH OF TIMBER FOR THE FRAME BASE, OR BUY A REBATED TIMBER MOULDING.

1 Measure and mark four 47 cm (19 in) lengths on the rebated timber. Mitre-cut the lengths and sand the edges. Make them up into a square frame, using a small amount of wood glue and a corrugated fixing across each corner.

2 Paint the frame base using milk paint in medium-blue. Leave to dry.

3 Place spindles against the frame and decide on the best features and where to place them. Mark these with a pencil.

4 Place each spindle in a vice and saw it into the required pieces. Arrange the pieces on the frame base. Blunt the ends of the panel pins by snipping them off with wire cutters, then apply a thin coating of wood glue to the joining surfaces and use pins to hold them in place.

5 Use a centre punch to push the heads of the pins well beneath the surface of the wood.

6 Distress the old paintwork, using a chisel and sandpaper to scuff up the surface. Apply a coat of antiquing varnish to the whole mirror frame. Have a mirror cut to the size of the rebate and attach with fixings.

MATERIALS AND EQUIPMENT YOU WILL NEED

2000 MM (6 FT 6 IN) PLANED TIMBER 45 x 18 MM (1¼ x ¾ IN) • RULER • PENCIL • MITRE BLOCK • TENON SAW • SANDPAPER • WOOD GLUE • CORRUGATED FIXINGS • HAMMER • MILK PAINT IN MEDIUM-BLUE • PAINTBRUSHES • 2 RECLAIMED OR NEW STAIRCASE SPINDLES • VICE • 40 MM (1½ IN) PANEL PINS • WIRE CUTTERS • CENTRE PUNCH • CHISEL • ANTIQUING VARNISH • MIRROR • FIXINGS

BOLTED COFFEE TABLE

THIS CHUNKY COFFEE TABLE USES A SIMPLE CONSTRUCTION METHOD FOR THE TOP, MAKING A STABLE FLAT SURFACE FROM TIMBER PLANKS WITHOUT THE NEED FOR GLUED JOINTS THAT REQUIRE SPECIAL CLAMPS. THE FIXINGS FOR THE TOP ARE NOT ONLY FUNCTIONAL BUT ALSO FORM A FEATURE OF THE DESIGN. THE LEGS ARE ATTACHED USING A SIMPLE TENON JOINT, BUT IF YOU DON'T WANT TO CUT THESE YOU COULD ACHIEVE THE SAME EFFECT BY GLUING EXTRA WOOD PANELS AROUND A CENTRAL CORE FOR EACH LEG. STAIN AND VARNISH THE TABLE, OR GIVE IT A SIMPLE FINISH WITH OIL AND WAX.

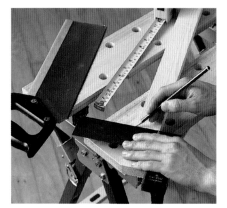

1 Mark the timber and cut to size, following the measurements shown on the working drawing.

3 Use the first batten as a guide for drilling all the remaining battens for the table top.

4 Assemble the top temporarily and mark the position of the legs 90 mm (3 in) in from the table edges.

2 Drill 12 mm (⅝ in) holes 63 mm (2½ in) from each end of each batten. Drill a third hole through the centre.

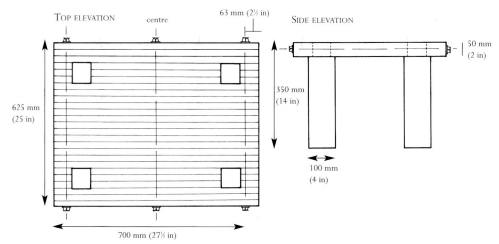

TOP ELEVATION   centre   63 mm (2½ in)

SIDE ELEVATION   50 mm (2 in)

625 mm (25 in)

350 mm (14 in)

700 mm (27½ in)

100 mm (4 in)

MATERIALS AND EQUIPMENT YOU WILL NEED

50 x 25 MM (2 x 1 IN) AND 100 MM (4 IN) SQUARE SOFTWOOD • PENCIL • MEASURING TAPE • TRY-SQUARE • TENON SAW • DRILL • G-CLAMP • 10 MM (½ IN) STUDDING • SANDPAPER • PENNY WASHERS • NUTS • SPANNER • HACKSAW • METAL FILE

5 Dismantle the table top and cut the marked battens to make the leg joint or mortice.

6 Mark out the positioning of the tenons on the legs.

7 Make all the vertical cuts first, cutting carefully to the marked lines using a tenon saw.

8 Turn each leg on its side and saw across to meet the vertical cuts.

9 Sand all the battens and the legs. Paint the legs as desired at this point.

10 Assemble the top again using the studding and insert the legs.

11 Tighten the studding, making sure you use washers between the nuts and the wood.

12 Use a hacksaw to trim off the excess studding and finally file the ends smooth.

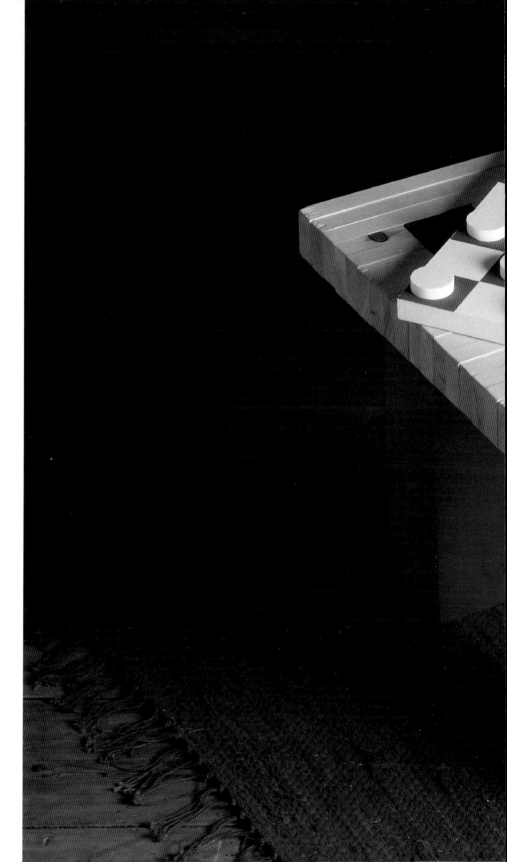

TOMATO DRAWERS

Supermarkets and food stores throw away tomato boxes every day, but you can recycle them to make this novel chest. When the boxes start to wear out or get dirty, just collect some more and replace them. You can paint or decorate the boxes if you want a change from tomatoes, and paint or varnish the frame as you wish. This chest is six drawers high, but you can adapt the frame to take any number of boxes.

1 Collect a set of matching boxes and measure them to calculate the size of the cabinet. If your boxes are the same size as those used here, you can use the measurements given on the plan provided.

2 Cut out all the timber, according to the working drawing that follows.

3 Drill holes in the ends of each cross rail, positioning them centrally.

▶

MATERIALS AND EQUIPMENT YOU WILL NEED

Tomato boxes • Measuring tape • 25 mm (1 in) square and 25 x 40 mm (1 x 1½ in) softwood • Tenon saw • Drill • Sandpaper • T-square • 40 mm (1½ in) screws • Screwdriver • Wood glue • Short nails • Hammer • Tinted varnish • Paintbrush

4 Sand all the frame components smooth.

6 Using wood glue and nails, attach runner guides to all the rails except the top one.

7 Lay the assembled frames side by side and attach the short cross rails. Turn over and repeat on the other side. When the glue is dry, give the whole frame a coat of tinted varnish.

5 Lay out two legs and assemble the first side, positioning the first cross rail one thickness of timber from the top. According to the size of your boxes, measure down from the first rail to find the position for the next rail on each side.

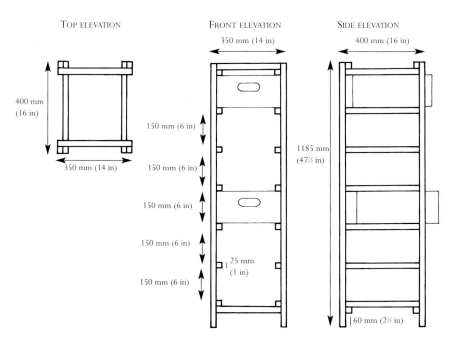

TOP ELEVATION

400 mm (16 in)

350 mm (14 in)

FRONT ELEVATION

350 mm (14 in)

150 mm (6 in)

150 mm (6 in)

150 mm (6 in)

150 mm (6 in)

25 mm (1 in)

150 mm (6 in)

SIDE ELEVATION

400 mm (16 in)

1185 mm (47½ in)

60 mm (2½ in)

TEMPLATES

THE MEASUREMENTS GIVEN FOR EACH TEMPLATE ARE THOSE USED WITHIN THE INDIVIDUAL PROJECTS. WHERE NO MEASUREMENTS ARE GIVEN, THEY ARE REPRODUCED AT THE SAME SIZE, OR AN ENLARGEMENT SIZE IS SPECIFIED. FOR AN ENLARGEMENT, EITHER USE A GRID SYSTEM OR PHOTOCOPIER.

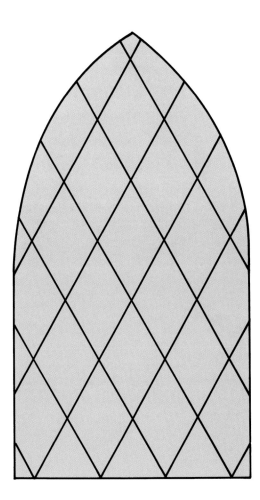

OSTRICH (SEE ZEBRA RODEO PP78—81)
ENLARGE ON PHOTOCOPIER BY 165% FOR EXACT SIZE.

HARLEQUIN BOOK END PP40—41
ENLARGE ON PHOTOCOPIER BY 200% FOR EXACT SIZE.

COUNTRY-STYLE PELMET PP62—63
ENLARGE ON PHOTOCOPIER BY 200% FOR EXACT SIZE.

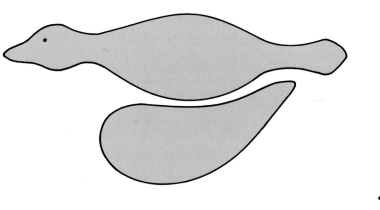

FLYING DUCKS PP54–55
ENLARGE ON PHOTOCOPIER BY 500% FOR EXACT SIZE.

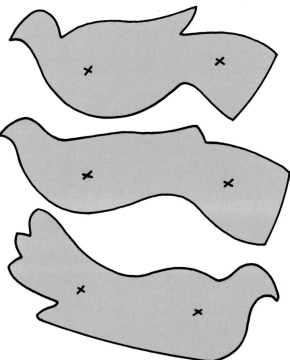

BIRD DRAWER HANDLES PP46–47
ENLARGE ON PHOTOCOPIER BY 200% FOR EXACT SIZE.

LONDON BUS PHOTOGRAPH FRAME PP64–65
ENLARGE ON PHOTOCOPIER BY 500% FOR EXACT SIZE.

MAPLE CLOCK PP34–36
USE RIGHT HAND COLUMN AT SAME SIZE
FOR MARQUETRY NUMBER PLAQUE PP48–50
ENLARGE APPROPRIATE NUMERALS ON PHOTOCOPIER BY
500% FOR EXACT SIZE.

SWEDISH POKERWORK CUPBOARD PP60–61

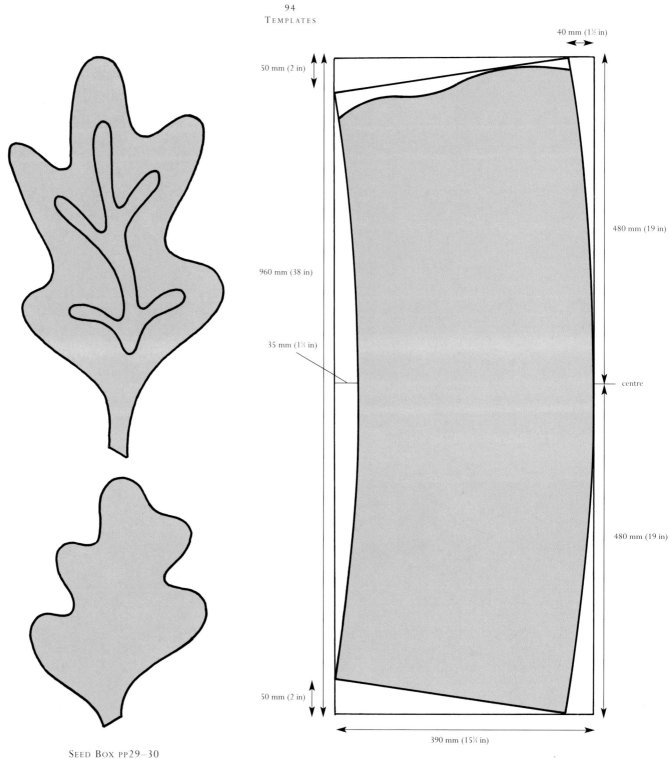

40 mm (1½ in)

50 mm (2 in)

480 mm (19 in)

960 mm (38 in)

35 mm (1⅜ in)

centre

480 mm (19 in)

50 mm (2 in)

390 mm (15¼ in)

SEED BOX PP29–30
ENLARGE BY 200% FOR EXACT SIZE.

WAVE WASTEPAPER BIN PP37–39

SUPPLIERS

United Kingdom

Axminster Power Tool Centre
Chard Street
Axminster
Devon EX13 5HU

John Boddy's Wood and Tool Store
Riverside Sawmills
Boroughbridge
North Yorkshire YO5 9LJ

Chestergate Wood Supplies Ltd
Porron Street, Portwood
Stockport
Greater Manchester SK1 2JD

Grampian Power Tools
Unit 4
Frederick Street Business Centre
Aberdeen AB24 5HY

Homecrafts Direct
PO Box 38
Leicester LE1 9BU
tel: 0116 251 3139

North Wales Timber Ltd
Industrial Estate
Pinfold Lane, Buckley
Flintshire CH7 3PL

West and Heaton Timber Ltd
4 North Back Lane
Bridlington
East Yorkshire YO16 5BA

JMJ Woodworking Machinery Ltd
Main Street, Skidby
Cottingham
East Yorkshire HU16 5TG

United States

Colonial Hardwoods Inc.
7953 Cameron Brown Ct
Springfield, VA 22153
tel: (703) 451-9217
www.colonialhardwoods@rica.com
Handloggers
135 E. Sir Francis Drake Blvd
Larkspur, CA 94939

Talarico Hardwoods
Route 3, Box 3268
Mohnton, PA 19540

Viking Woodcrafts Inc.
1317 8th Street SE
Waseca, MN 56093
tel: (507) 835-8043
www.vikingwoodrafts.com

Woodcrafts & Supplies
405 East Indiana Street
Oblong, IL 62449
tel: (800) 592-4907
www.woodcraftssupplies.com

Wood to Paint
P.O. Box 70
Mound, MN 55364
tel: (800) 441-9870

Australia

Anagote Timbers
144 Renwick Street, Marrickville
New South Wales 2204
tel: 02 9558 8444

Trend Timbers Pty Ltd
Cunneen Street, McGraths Hill
New South Wales 2756
tel: 02 4577 5277

The Wood Works

8 Railway Road, Meadowbank
New South Wales 2114
tel: 02 9807 7244

Lazarides Timber Agencies
PO Box 440, Ferny Hills
Queensland 4055
tel: 07 3851 1400

Veneers
37 Alexandra Road, East Ringwood,
Victoria 3135
tel: 03 9870 8733

PUBLISHER'S ACKNOWLEDGEMENTS

A big thank you to the authors Sally and Stewart Walton for their inspirational projects (pages 24, 26, 28, 31, 42, 46, 51, 56, 72 and 82).

Many thanks also to the project contributors: Penny Boylan, page 44; Jason Cleverly, pages 66 and 78; Lucinda Ganderton, pages 40, 54, 60, 62 and 76; Andrew Gillmore, pages 34, 37, 48, 64, 69, 84 and 88.

Also to the wood artists who kindly contributed work to the Gallery: Fiona Clark (tel: 0171 729 7079), Jason Cleverly (tel: 01782 610192), Andrew Gillmore (c/o Publishers), Carl Hahn (tel: 01548 550861), Nicola Henshaw (tel: 0171 627 8747), Walter Jack (tel: 0117 939 3336), James Marston (tel: 01308 420631), Malcolm Martin (c/o Publishers), Lynn Muir (01288 361561), Kathryn O'Kell (tel: 01562 637729) and Jeff Soan (tel: 0181 691 1332).

Thank you to Peter Williams and Georgina Rhodes, the photographer and stylist, for their magical project shots. And to Rodney Forte for

the step-by-step photography.

Grateful thanks to The Pier, 200 Tottenham Court Road, London W19 0AD for the loan of props.

AUTHORS' ACKNOWLEDGEMENTS

Thankyou to Adrian at Stamco, our local timber merchants in St Leonards-on-Sea, for his help, wit and wisdom; Douglas and Pauline for the use of their carpentry shed; and Homecrafts Direct and The Old Village Paint Store for providing materials and equipment.

Picture credits

Thank you to the following agencies and museums for permission to reproduce pictures in this book: page 8, British Museum, London/ Bridgeman Art Library (left); Musée des Arts d'Afrique et d'Oceanie/ Bridgeman Art Library (centre); British Museum/E.T. Archive (right); page 9 (both pictures), Victoria & Albert Museum, London/Bridgeman Art Library.

INDEX

animal print boxes, 44–5
automata, zebra rodeo, 78–81

balsa wood, mosaic keepsake, 24–5
bench, five-board, 72–5
bench hooks, 21
bench stops, 21
birds: drawer handles, 46–7
    flying ducks, 54–5
blades, sharpening, 22
boards, manufactured, 16
bolted coffee table, 84–7
book end, harlequin, 40–1
boxes:
    animal print boxes, 44–5
    seed box, 28–30
boxwood, fruitbox lampbase, 42–3
bus photograph frame, 64–5

carving, 8–9
    chip carved frame, 51–3
    fish hook, 26–7
    flying ducks, 54–5
    maple clock, 34–6
chest, tomato drawers, 88–90
chip carved frame, 51–3
chisels, 22
clamping wood, 21
Clark, Fiona, 11
Cleverly, Jason, 12
clock, maple, 34–6
coffee table, bolted, 84–7
contemporary shelf, 31–3
coping saws, 21
country–style pelmet, 62–3
crates, fruitbox lampbase, 42–3
cupboards:
    fish face cupboard, 66–8

    Swedish pokerwork cupboard, 60–1
curtain rail, rainforest, 76–7

display stand, 69–71
drawers:
    bird drawer handles, 46–7
    tomato drawers, 88–90
drawings, working, 23
drilling, guide holes, 21
ducks, flying, 54–5

equipment, 18–19

fish:
    fish face cupboard, 66–8
    fish hook, 26–7
five-board bench, 72–5
flying ducks, 54–5
frames:
    chip carved frame, 51–3
    London bus photograph frame, 64–5
    spindle frame, 82–3
fruitbox lampbase, 42–3

Gillmore, Andrew, 12
guide holes, 21

Hahn, Carl, 14
handles, bird, 46–7
hardwoods, 16
harlequin book end, 40–1
Henshaw, Nicola, 13
history, 8–9
hook, fish, 26–7

Jack, Walter, 12

keepsake, mosaic, 24–5
knives, scoring with, 20

lampbase, fruitbox, 42–3
lathes, 9
London bus photograph frame, 64–5

maple clock, 34–6
marking out, 20
marquetry, 9
    number plate, 48–50
Marston, James, 11
Martin, Malcolm, 15
materials, 16–17
MDF, 16
    bird drawer handles, 46–7
    fruitbox lampbase, 42–3
mirror, spindle frame, 82–3
model townscape, 56–9
mosaic keepsake, 24–5
mouldings, panel pins, 23
Muir, Lynn, 15

number plate, marquetry, 48–50

obeche wood, chip carved frame, 51–3
O'Kell, Kathryn, 14

painting:
    country-style pelmet, 62–3
    fish face cupboard, 66–8
    harlequin book end, 40–1
    model townscape, 56–9
    rainforest curtain rail, 76–7
panel pins, 23
pelmet, country–style, 62–3
photograph frame, London bus, 64–5
pine, 16
    country-style pelmet, 62–3
    fish face cupboard, 66–8
    five-board bench, 72–5
    flying ducks, 54–5
    harlequin book end, 40–1
    model townscape, 56–9
planes, 22
plywood, 16
    display stand, 69–71
    London bus photograph frame, 64–5
    wave wastepaper bin, 37–9
    zebra rodeo, 78–81
poker work see pyrography
poplar wood, fish hook, 26–7
pyrography, 9
    animal print boxes, 44–5
    rainforest curtain rail, 76–7
    Swedish pokerwork cupboard, 60–1

rainforest curtain rail, 76–7
recycled timber, 16
    contemporary shelf, 31–3
    fruitbox lampbase, 42–3
    spindle frame, 82–3

sanding blocks, 22
saws, 18, 21
scoring, 20
seed box, 28–30
sharpening blades, 22
shelf, contemporary, 31–3
Soan, Jeff, 10
softwoods, 16
spindle frame, 82–3
stand, display, 69–71
Swedish pokerwork cupboard, 60–1

table, bolted, 84–7
techniques, 20–3
templates, 91–4
tenon saws, 21
tomato drawers, 88–90
tools, 18–19
townscape, model, 56–9
toys, zebra rodeo, 78–81
turning, 9
    spindle frame, 82–3

varnishing, 23
veneers, marquetry number plate, 48–50

wave wastepaper bin, 37–9
woodburning, 9
    animal print boxes, 44–5
    rainforest curtain rail, 76–7
    Swedish pokerwork cupboard, 60–1
working drawings, 23

zebra rodeo, 78–81